Walther Ziegler

Kant

in 60 Minutes

Translated by

Alexander Reynolds

My thanks go to Rudolf Aichner for his tireless critical editing; Silke Ruthenberg for the fine graphics; Lydia Pointvogl, Eva Amberger, Christiane Hüttner, and Dr. Martin Engler for their excellent work as manuscript readers and sub-editors; Prof. Guntram Knapp, who first inspired me with enthusiasm for philosophy; and Angela Schumitz, who handled in the most professional manner, as chief editorial reader, the production of both the German and the English editions of this series of books.

My special thanks go to my translator

Dr Alexander Reynolds.

Himself a philosopher, he not only translated the original German text into English with great care and precision but also, in passages where this was required in order to ensure clear understanding, supplemented this text with certain formulations adapted specifically to the needs of English-language readers.

Two things fill the mind with ever new and increasing admiration and reverence the more often and steadily one reflects on them: *the starry heavens above me and the moral law within me.* [1]

Bibliographic Information held by the German National Library: The details of the original German edition of this publication are held by the German National Library as part of the German National Bibliography; detailed bibliographical data can be found online at www.dnb.de.

Publisher and Printing:
BoD – Books on Demand, Norderstedt
ISBN 9783741226373

Contents

Kant's Great Discovery

Immanuel Kant is thought to be perhaps the greatest of all philosophers. And Kant did make, in the 18th Century, two great discoveries which engage us still today. Firstly, he founded the globally acknowledged 'categorical imperative' in moral philosophy; secondly, he became the first philosopher to succeed in answering that question as old as humanity of how knowledge arises in our brains. In his main work, the 1000-page *Critique of Pure Reason*, Kant analysed the working of Man's thinking apparatus.

Kant was prompted to this analysis by noting that all philosophers before him had defended different views and had even arrived at knowledge-claims directly opposed to one another:

Philosophy is swarming with mistaken definitions [...]. [2]

This was due, in Kant's view, to an improper use of the faculty of reason. All human beings, indeed – and thus all philosophers, too – perceive the same reality. If philosophers, then, had arrived at conflicting opinions this was caused, Kant believed, by illusions and errors in thinking. So as not to fall himself into such errors, Kant decided, midway through his career, to refrain for a time from making any philosophical claims. For eleven years he published nothing: no book, no essay, not a single word – although in fact, as a university professor of philosophy, regular publication was expected of him. Instead, he withdrew, at age forty-six, into his study and began tenaciously to research the question of how exactly the apparatus of thinking functions and of how we should apply it if we are to arrive at error-free statements about reality. He critically examined what human beings *can* gain knowledge of by applying the faculty of reason and what they *cannot* gain knowledge of, since it lies outside the jurisdiction of this faculty. This was why Kant gave to his main work the title: *Critique of Pure Reason.*

> Yet by this I do not understand a critique of books and systems but a critique of the faculty of reason in general [...]. [3]

The decisive question for Kant was always the single critical one: what can reason truly know with certainty and where does mere speculation begin?

He sought the answer to this question as if possessed. He got his servant to wake him up every morning at five with the words: "It is time!" Still in his nightgown, he worked for two hours at his writing desk before going to give his daily university lecture between seven and nine. Then he returned to his desk and wrote for the rest of the morning before taking his midday meal, exactly at noon, with friends. He forbade, however, discussion of philosophy during the meal, as he needed an hour's distraction in order to continue to work with concentration through the afternoon. He was so punctual in taking, at five, his daily constitutional that it was said that the citizens of Königsberg set their clocks by him as he left his house with hat and walking stick. The evening hours he spent reading the works of other philosophers before retiring, with equal punctuality, at ten o'clock to bed. It was in this way that he confronted, day by day, month by month and year by year, tirelessly and with iron discipline, the key question: how does human reason function and what can human beings know by reason's application?

Kant pondered in this way – with a patience that is

almost inconceivable for us today – for eleven long years before he finally gave his answer to the world. It was worthy of the long effort. His *Critique of Pure Reason* became a sensation. Once its difficult content had been grasped, the book became famous all over the world and it is still considered to be the most important work of philosophy ever written. But it also got Kant into trouble with the Church. For the result of his labours was one very hard for believers to accept. The critical investigation of the human thinking apparatus (or, as Kant put it, of 'pure reason') forces us to conclude that our capacity for knowledge is very limited. Our reason, Kant contends, can provide true and certain knowledge only of that which we have already perceived through our five senses (i.e. seen, heard, smelt, tasted, or touched). Nobody can arrive at a truly sure and reliable knowledge of an object merely by thinking and meditating upon it if he has never perceived this object through his senses. God counts, for Kant, among this class of objects that cannot be known, since He can never become the object of an 'intuition'. (This term – 'Anschauung' in Kant's German – was used rather differently in Kant's day than in ours. Today intuition has an almost metaphysical connotation ('female intuition' etc), but in Kant's day it meant perception through sight and the other physical senses. For this reason, we shall, below, mostly use 'sense-perception' to render it into English.) Although we use the word 'God', no one has ever seen Him. God, consequently, is initially only an abstract thought or, as Kant puts it, an 'empty concept':

Thoughts without content are empty [...]. [4]

This was why Kant rejected all philosophical proofs of God's existence as unscientific, although such proofs were widespread in his day. Neither God nor the Devil nor life after death can, Kant concluded, possibly be known or proven by reason. Such conclusions, of course, earned him the enmity of the established churches. The devout Prussian king Frederick William II strictly forbade him to teach or disseminate these views on God and religion. For many years, no professor in Prussia was allowed to lecture on Kant's critical writings about religion.

But the service that Kant did the natural sciences with his 'critique of knowledge' was truly inestimable. He gave researchers, for the first time, a set of logical tools which was sensationally simple and yet quite perfect, and that still remains valid today and makes all scientific results achieved worldwide mutually comparable. Every theory, Kant argued, however good, must be proven in terms of actual sense-perceptions, for example through repeatable experiments. Only when so proven can it count as true knowledge. Thus began that triumphant progress of the natural sciences and technology which still continues today. Research results could now be checked, compared and further developed worldwide, since all researchers employed the same epistemologically-guaranteed method, namely, Kant's. By being the first to answer the epistemological question: 'What can I know?' Kant prepared the ground for the great global flowering of scientific endeavour.

But this was by no means all. In his second major work, the *Critique of Practical Reason*, Kant tackles what is perhaps an even more important question for mankind:

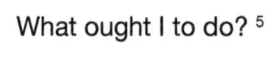

What ought I to do? [5]

Life is not just about investigating and knowing the world but above all about behaving rightly in it and doing good, not evil. But what is good and what is evil? How ought one to behave? Is there a way of acting which is generally and equally right for all human beings?

Kant succeeded in developing a sensational answer also to this question: the so-called 'categorical imperative'. Still today, two hundred years after Kant formulated it, millions of school and university students all over the world learn this maxim of moral action. The contrast between the vastness of Kant's influence on the world and the modesty of the life he lived is striking. It is said that he never once left the area of his small native city of Königsberg (now Kaliningrad). A contemporary biographer relates that he only once ventured a few miles, by horse-drawn coach, outside the city limits in order to visit a friend. But the unusually late homecoming proved such a disturbance to his daily routine that he resolved never to indulge in such 'adventures' again and to devote himself exclusively to his studies. Women had absolutely no place in his life. He considered them to be a waste of time and a potential distraction from higher things. When questioned about his lifelong bachelorhood he would say:

Woman becomes free by marriage; man loses his freedom by it. [6]

Kant really had only one pleasure: thought – and the indulgence he permitted himself here was boundless. Both his contemporaries and many later thinkers have noted with amusement the almost compulsive quality that Kant brought to 'the simple life'. But the incontestable fact remains that this obsessive self-discipline yielded the most significant and enduring ethical vision that mankind has ever produced: the categorical imperative. The categorical imperative is timeless and modern above all because Kant proposed here, for the first time, a principle for right action based exclusively on reason and not, as in earlier times, on a belief in good and evil *per se*.

With Kant there entered an entirely new kind of thinking into the history of philosophy and of mankind: namely, critical thinking. Kant, we may say, was perhaps the most consistent representative of the Enlightenment inasmuch as he urged people to self-critically examine all their own claims to knowledge and to thoroughly free themselves from all the apparent knowledge handed down to them by tradition:

> Enlightenment is the human being's emergence from his self-incurred minority. [7]

(The Cambridge Edition of Kant's writings uses the rather old-fashioned term 'minority' here as a translation of Kant's *Unmuendigkeit*. The term does not refer to a 'minority' in the sense opposed to a 'majority' but rather to the *condition of being a minor*, or being a child subject to tutelage).

Kant's Central Idea

What Can I Know?
The Critique of Pure Reason

Kant once stated in one of his philosophical lectures that there are, in philosophy, really only four questions of any true importance: 'what can I know?'; 'what ought I to do?'; 'what may I hope?'; and 'what is Man?' He engaged above all with the first two of these four questions.

The fundamental question of what a human being can know is investigated by Kant in his mighty thousand-page masterwork, the *Critique of Pure Reason*. As in the case of 'intuition', we should take note of a change in the meaning of the word 'critique' between Kant's day and ours. Today, 'critique' implies a negative judgment; but Kant uses it rather in the original sense of the Greek word it comes from: *'krinein'*, which means 'investigate' or 'examine'. He wants to investigate what pure reason can and cannot do. He compares this critical examination to a court trial at which reason is at the same time prosecutor and accused, inasmuch as it is (self-)compelled to examine, (self-)critically, its own capacities. Kant believed such a rigorous 'trial' to be, after two thousand years of philosophy, long overdue; the philosophers' centuries-old discussion about truth was threatening, he thought, to sink into contradictions and chaos and the age itself now demanded that

[...] reason take on anew the most difficult of all its tasks, namely, that of self-knowledge, and institute a court of justice by which reason may secure its rightful claims while dismissing all its groundless pretensions [...] and this court is none other than the critique of pure reason itself. [8]

It is clear from these last remarks just how vast an undertaking Kant envisaged. He is not concerned with any new philosophical or scientific theory but with something much more fundamental. His intent is to examine just what, where human reason is applied correctly, can, in theory, be known and what cannot possibly be known.

Hence it is the first and most important occupation of philosophy to deprive dialectic once and for all of all disadvantageous influence, by blocking off the source of the errors. [9]

The source of these errors is, Kant contends, a lack of knowledge of the apparatus itself of human thinking. Too often in the past, and still today, this apparatus of thinking is applied in the wrong way. Kant wants, as he stresses over and over again, to establish 'once and for all' – that is to say, for all times past and future – a foundation for any science really worthy of the name 'science'. He wants to clarify just what we are really talking about when we talk about 'scientific knowledge'.

The Dispute between Rationalists and Empiricists

In Kant's time there existed two major currents in philosophical thought: rationalism and empiricism. These two schools of thought were deeply at odds, with the rationalists condemning the empiricists as naïve and the empiricists the rationalists as narrow-minded dogmatists.

The rationalists drew their name from the Latin word ratio, which does in fact mean simply 'reason'. And it was indeed on reason alone that these philosophers built all their accounts of truth and the world. It was only with the aid of reason, they argued – that is to say, through rational contemplation and the process of logical conclusion – that true insights were arrived at. It was just such a decisive and even exclusive role in the discovery of truth that was assigned to reason by the famous dictum of the French rationalist, Descartes: "I think, therefore I am."

For these advocates of reason, then, nothing else that human beings might base their ideas about the world on – for example, what we perceive through our five senses – is really sufficient to arrive at truth.

Take, for example, the rising of the sun. To believe that the sun rises merely because one sees it do so every morning might well be to fall victim to an optical illusion. Looked at in rationalist terms – that is to say, purely logically – the proposition 'the sun rises' is quite false. In these terms it would be more correct to say that in the morning the earth turns toward the sun and in the evening away from it. It might also sometimes be erroneous to claim that someone is big simply because he appears to cut an imposing figure. In comparison to others he may be small. The decisive thing, then – so it might be argued – is not what we perceive about a thing or a person through our senses but rather the rational idea 'relation' and the logical inferences that follow from it. *Ratio* – reason – alone, being the competent faculty for logical comparisons, can decide whether someone is big or small, or whether it is the sun that 'rises' or the earth that 'turns' toward the sun. True statements, the rationalists contended, were only possible where reason applied the logic of comparative or causal thought.

The rationalists, then, wanted to explain the whole world through logical deductions alone. In this way, they also claimed knowledge of such metaphysical truths as the existence of God. They reasoned, for example, as follows: if the movements of the world or of nature consist in a long sequence of causes and effects, then it follows logically that there must have been a First Cause, or 'Prime Mover', that set everything in motion without itself being set in motion by anything else, i.e. stands outside of the chain of natural cause and effect. It was nothing unusual for the rationalists – who included, besides Descartes, such still well-known figures as Spinoza and Leibniz – to offer such 'proofs of God's existence' on purely logical grounds.

Empiricism claimed the exact opposite to this: namely, that it is not thinking but rather experience – that is to say, the perception of the world through our five senses – that is the only reliable source of truth. The empiricists took their name from the Latin word 'empiricus': 'following experience'. They were fascinated by the natural sciences, just beginning to flourish at this time, and their experiments. They shared the sentiment of Goethe's Faust that 'all theory is grey' and that living knowledge is acquired by looking at things with one's own eyes and holding only to the concretely perceptible. The spirit of bold experimentation even cost one of the fathers of the empiricist current, Francis Bacon, his life. It is said that he died of pneumonia while trying to establish whether snow could be used to keep a dead fowl fresh.

Such a demise, however, only brought Bacon greater honour in the eyes of the empiricists. Their motto was: knowledge of Nature and its laws is to be gathered only from data acquired through the physical senses. They envisaged human reason as a vessel which is, at each man's birth, completely empty and which absorbs only as life progresses ever more images, impressions and experiences. Thus, for example, the child will only become aware that fire is hot once he has burned his fingers; he then stores this painful experience away in his understanding and is more careful in future. Perhaps the key statement of empiricism is the one attributed to the English empiricist John Locke "There is nothing in the mind that was not first in the senses". This was why the empiricists looked on rationalism, with its meditations on God, the Good, justice and other 'eternal truths', as mere speculation ; all experience gained through the senses was lacking here. 'Eternal truths', indeed, were simply impossible on this view, since every day brought new perceptions, experiments and experiences. Empiricism gained especially wide acceptance in Britain. We have mentioned the Englishmen Locke and Bacon. Other well-known empiricists active in the British Isles were Hobbes, Berkeley and Hume.

Kant's Brilliant Solution to the 'Problem of Knowledge'

Who, then, was right: the rationalists or the empiricists? Kant felt torn between the two positions. On the one hand, as a professor of philosophy, he shared the rationalists' interest in metaphysics: that science of pure mind which is defined as lying 'beyond physics'; he also sincerely wanted, as did the rationalists, to formulate viable ideas of such things as 'justice', 'right action', 'freedom', and 'the immortality of the soul'. What disturbed him, however, was the rationalists' speculative and contradictory way of reasoning, exemplified above all by their so-called 'proofs of God'. This prompted Kant to mistrust the rationalists and even to describe them as mere 'dogmatists' who shook, like stage conjurors, 'pseudo-proofs' out of their sleeves:

Thus, if one sees the dogmatist step forth with ten proofs, one can be sure that he has none at all. [10]

On the other hand, however, Kant also felt uncomfortable with empiricism. He lived, indeed, in an age highly attentive to the prospects recently opened up by the physics of Newton and recognized the huge progress which he, Copernicus, Kepler and Galileo had made thanks to the empirical method. He knew that the precise empirical observation of natural phenomena, such as the movement of the planets, had enriched human knowledge. But he also saw that the most successful among the physicists had often initially conceived their theories in their minds alone, in purely logical, rational, or even mathematical terms, and had only afterward compared these conceptions with observable events in Nature. And so Kant came to pose the central question: 'does one, as the empiricists claim, arrive at knowledge only *after* perceiving through the senses – that is, only *a posteriori*, to use the technical Latin term meaning 'afterward' – or can one possess or acquire knowledge *before* any sense-perception – or *a priori*, to use the Latin term meaning 'prior to' – that is, through thinking alone:

It is, therefore, at least a question requiring closer investigation [...] whether there is any such cognition independent of all experience and even of all impressions of the senses. One calls such cognitions a priori and distinguishes them from empirical ones, which have their sources a posteriori, namely in experience. [11]

(The Cambridge Edition of Kant's writings that is quoted in this book uses – as the reader will have noted – a slightly technical, Latin-based language. For example, what is called 'cognition' in the passage above would be called, in ordinary English, just 'knowing'. The English version differs in this respect from Kant's original German which used, for ideas like 'knowing', the same word as an ordinary German speaker would use. Nevertheless, in order to keep the language of this book in line with the language of the Kant editions quoted, we shall from now on use, besides the common term 'knowledge, also the more technical terms 'cognition' and 'cognitive' for the ideas 'knowing' and 'knowledge-related'.)

Kant also describes these *a priori* acts of cognition supposedly performed by the faculty of reason prior to any actual experience as acts of 'pure reason'. This is another reason why his main work is called the *Critique of Pure Reason*; it sets out to examine whether the human thinking apparatus 'pure and simple' can indeed, as the rationalists contended, produce knowledge ("cognition") without recourse to any sense-perception.

Kant's answer to the question 'who is right: the rationalists or the empiricists?' was as simple as it was brilliant. Kant said simply: 'We need both: on the one hand, the empirical, *a posteriori* perception provided by our senses, and on the other hand the *a priori* capacity of our understanding to think, categorize, and pass judgments. If contribution from either one of these two sides is lacking, real knowledge is not achieved. For in the one case our perceptions remain 'blind' and the impressions made on our senses cannot be further processed; and in the other our thoughts remain 'empty' because they have nothing concrete to hold onto:

> Without sensibility no object would be given to us, and without understanding none would be thought.

Thoughts without content are empty; intuitions without concepts are blind. [12]

(Once again, the reader should not be misled by the language used in the standard English edition of Kant, which is not so much technical as outdated. The term 'sensibility' has a long and complex history in English. Often it awakens, today, in ordinary English speakers the idea of 'over-sensitivity'. But in fact Kant means by it simply 'perception through the senses'. In the text, then, we shall use 'sense-perception' for this idea even if the quoted passages sometimes use 'sensibility'.)

Whoever has grasped this proposition has, basically, grasped the whole of the *Critique of Pure Reason*, since it contains the core and kernel of Kant's great discovery: any claim to scientific knowledge – indeed any claim to knowledge of any sort – must, if it is to count as credible and reliable, 'stand', as it were, 'on two legs': namely, on the one hand on direct perception through the eyes, ears and other sense-organs and, on the other hand, on the application of the logical concepts making up the apparatus of thought.

Let us take a first simple example of the need for *a posteriori* sense-perception and *a priori* conceptual thought to work together.

Empirical experience no more suffices in itself than does pure thinking. Let us imagine an early forebear of Stone Age Man: one who had perhaps just recently learned to walk upright but had, as yet, not developed intelligence. He is still at an archaic stage of development, in transition from animal to man, or even a little before that. He lives purely by instinct according to his sense-impressions alone and has not yet formed any logical cognitive categories.

If one were to take him out of this early quasi-animal phase and let him observe how a housewife prepares a pancake using yeast, he would surely have great difficulty understanding just what is going on. Being unable to think in terms of causal logic, he would have no chance of understanding why previously isolated yeast bacteria, once added to the mix, cause dough to rise by a process of fermentation, nor why the still-liquid dough gains solidity, warmth and a fragrant brown surface through being placed in a pan over an ignited flame. He would indeed see before him the flour, the added milk, the yeast and the frying pan, and perhaps even smell the delicious scent of the browned pancake; but, despite this wealth of sense-perceptions, he would, we must presume, never arrive at the knowledge: "Here, a pancake is being made with leavened dough."

This is because, as Kant argued, perceptions through the senses – be it of sight, smell, touch or hearing – produce, without the concepts of the understanding, no knowledge. If we cannot link these perceptions up to such concepts, we remain, despite this great wealth of different perceptual data, groping in the dark, or (as Kant himself puts it):

[...] Intuitions without concepts are blind. [13]

It is not until we apply to these intuitions (i.e. sense-perceptions) our apparatus of conceptual thought that we are able to form what we have perceived through our senses into actual knowledge. True knowledge always requires both: sense-perceptions on the one hand; mental concepts on the other. Where either is lacking, there can be no true knowledge.

We would be just as helpless, on the other hand, if we had only the concept 'leavened-dough pancake' but no sense-perception relating to it. If, for example, someone were to whisper just the abstract concept *naleshniki* into our ear, it might be that we would find ourselves unable to associate any sense-perceptions, either from memory or from present experience, with this sequence of sounds. We would be able to make no sense of this concept *naleshniki*. Or, as Kant would say, the concept would remain, in this case, 'empty'.

It would be only on being told that *naleshniki* is the Polish word for 'pancake', so that our thinking apparatus begins to connect with this concept the actually experienced sense-perception of a tasty flour-based dish with cinnamon and sugar, that this concept would acquire a meaning for us. For Kant, then, knowledge is a process which, by application of the understanding, orders raw sense-impressions into concepts. It is for this reason that every true cognition – every case of real 'knowing' – must 'stand on two legs': the perceiving senses and the understanding. The following diagram clarifies Kant's concept of human cognition:

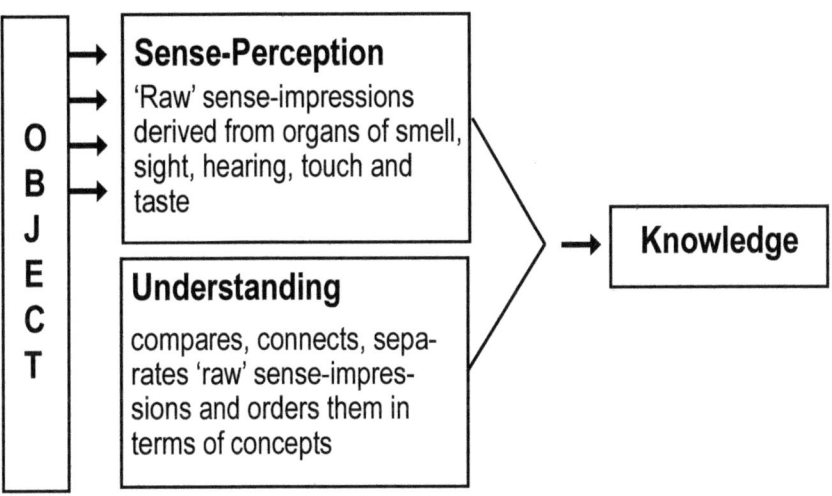

It is to the detailed description of this doubly-sourced process of human cognition that Kant devotes the hundreds of pages of his *Critique of Pure Reason*. Indeed, he does not just describe it; he provides reasons why the human thought-apparatus cannot be conceived of in any other way. The problem that Kant tackles is that of defining the conditions to which every possible act of human cognition must necessarily conform. He poses, therefore, the question: 'how does our thought-apparatus need to be constituted in order for something like 'perception' to be possible at all?' This method of proceeding he calls 'transcendental philosophy'.

Space and Time

Here we get into the meat of the problem. Kant now proceeds to show us, in detail, all that must occur, in each fraction of a second, within the human thought-apparatus in order, in the end, for something like cognition – i.e. knowing something to be true – to be possible:

There is no doubt whatever that all our cognition begins with experience, for how else should the cognitive faculty be awakened into exercise if not through objects that stimulate our senses and in part themselves produce representations, in part

bring the activity of our understanding into motion to compare these, to connect or separate them and thus to work up the raw material of sensible impressions into a cognition of objects that is called experience? [15]

Here, Kant says three important things. Firstly, he repeats that every 'cognition' begins with the objects which impinge on our senses, i.e. with sense-perception:

> [...]for how else should the cognitive faculty be awakened into exercise if not through objects that stimulate our senses [...]. [16]

Secondly, he describes, very beautifully, the work of our thought-apparatus as an 'activity of our understanding' consisting in the 'working-up' and ordering, by means of 'comparisons, connections and separations', of the raw material of our sense-impressions:

> [...] the activity of our understanding [...] to compare these (sense-impressions), to connect or separate them [...]. [17]

And thirdly, he adds an interesting further remark: Experiences, writes Kant, are nothing other than simple cognitions:

> [...](working up) the raw material of sensible impressions into a cognition of objects that is called experience [...]. [18]

The process that Kant calls 'cognition', then, does not occur only as organized scientific research but every day in the head of every human being because we have experiences almost every minute of our lives – for example, when we hear the alarm-clock ring, smell the coffee, get out of bed and search for our keys after breakfast to go to work. Even such small daily experiences as these are 'cognitions', 'acts of knowing'. Our apparatus of thought – or, as Kant says, our 'cognitive faculty' – is active at every moment and is constantly forming little 'cognitions' out of the 'raw material of sensible impressions', simply by 'comparing, connecting and separating' these impressions.

Thus the racket in one's ear every morning is compared, by the understanding, with various possible concepts, separated off from those that don't fit, and finally connected with the concept 'alarm-clock'. And from this conceptual cognition there is immediately drawn the further conclusion that it is time to get up.

The other 'raw sense-impressions' are likewise 'worked up' by the cognitive apparatus with lightning speed. I smell something, connect it with the scent of fresh-brewed coffee, and conclude that someone is already in the kitchen. I hear a chirping, connect this with the concept 'birds', and note that the birds are louder than usual. I am blinded by bright light and recognize, after a while, that the curtain is slightly open. I connect this bright light with the concept 'sun'. But that is not all. My cognitive apparatus goes on with its lightning-fast activity and draws the following conclusion from effect back to cause: the sun is blinding me, and the birds are singing particularly loudly; therefore the day must be clear and cloudless. And from this in turn the further conclusion: if the weather does not change, it will be very hot, so I should wear only t-shirt and shorts.

A great deal, then, has occurred in a split second. In the brief moment after waking, my cognitive apparatus has assigned the 'raw sensations'provided by my senses of hearing, sight, smell and touch to the four concepts 'alarm-clock', 'sun', 'coffee' and 'birds' and then gone on to form from these concepts the causal sequence: 'early morning, birds singing – blinding sunlight – hot day – shorts'. But *how* exactly has all this occurred? What exactly enters the brain from outside it and how is it 'worked up' there? How do 'raw sense-impressions' give rise to simple thoughts and these in turn to scientific cognitions?

For Kant, everything begins with 'raw sense-impressions'. First, I hear, smell, or see something. Thus far, then, Kant agrees with the empiricists. But in the same moment something else happens that the empiricists completely overlooked. With lightning speed I slip over my sound- and sight-impressions a kind of spatio-temporal grid – and this grid is something which I have already (that is, *a priori*) in my head. This grid is not, as the empiricists say, to be found in the external world; rather, it is located, already prior to all experience, within each person's cognitive apparatus. The moment I open my eyes, I am already applying this grid. I relentlessly force each sense-impression into a spatio-temporal 'corset'. I see, for example, the alarm-clock directly in front of me; a yard beyond the clock I see the window; and an inch or two in front of the window the hanging curtain, with a four-inch gap between its two halves that allows a ray of sunlight to pass into the room. My perception of each thing, in other words, involves grouping this thing with or against other things in terms of distances, spaces and positional relations like 'in front of', 'beyond', 'above' and 'below':

> [...] in order for me to represent them as outside one another, thus not merely as different but as in different places, the representation of space must already be their ground. [19]

If my cognitive apparatus orders sense-impressions, generally and instantaneously, into a spatial grid in this way, it also orders them, equally generally and instantaneously, into a temporal grid, or temporal sequence. First, I hear only the ringing of the alarm-clock and then, once this ringing has ceased, the song of the birds. Almost simultaneously with hearing the birdsong I smell the scent of the coffee. And a few moments later I feel the sun-rays on my half-opened, blinking eyes. Kant argues, then, that we cannot help but organize the things we perceive into spatial and temporal categories; this type of perception, he says, is irremovably built into our cognitive apparatus. And since this feeling for space and time exists in us *a priori* – that is to say, from the very start and prior to all experience – it is clearly not from any empirical sense-perception – that is, from any *a posteriori* experience acquired only in the course of seeing, touching etc. – that we acquire it. In other words, 'space' is not anything that we can perceive, just by using our eyes, to exist in the exterior world; rather, it is a cognitive horizon which limits and organizes every possible idea that we can form of the things that make up this world; for a thing to be 'visible' at all means that it is *already* enclosed by this horizon and appears against its background or (as Kant says) on its 'ground':

Space is a necessary representation a priori which is the ground of all outer intuitions (sense-impressions). [20]

The proof that Kant offers for this thesis is a negative one: he challenges the reader to envisage an object that would neither have spatial extension nor be located at any specific point in space. This, he says, is impossible. I can form the idea of an individual book in all sorts of spatial situations: on a bookshelf; lying on a table; as part of a library, or even floating in outer space; but some sort of spatial dimension will always be part of my idea of it; I cannot 'think away' spatiality itself:

One can never represent that there is no space, although one can very well think that there are no objects to be encountered in it. [21]

I can, of course, by an act of imagination, remove even this object 'book' from the space I am imagining and envisage a room fitted out as a library but entirely empty. But even in such a case the idea 'space' is maintained. Kant offers many more arguments for his thesis that our spatial perception is *a priori*, i.e. an abstract grid which we slip over all perceived objects in the moment of perceiving them. He stresses repeatedly that this spatial grid is to be found within oneself, not in the external world.

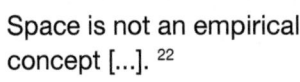 

Space is not an empirical concept [...]. [22]

For example, argues Kant, no one is able to actually empirically perceive 'space in its entirety', that is to say, a general space in which all concrete spaces are comprised:

[...] if one speaks of many spaces, one understands by that only parts of one and the same unique space. And these parts [...] are only thought *in it*. [23]

We can, indeed, visually perceive certain concrete spaces – such as a room, or a large hall, or even the vast space comprised within the dome of a cathedral empirically. But we can never empirically perceive 'space' *per se* – i.e. that general dimension of spatiality in which all the perceptible cathedrals and smaller spaces of the world and the universe take their place. That is to say, the general idea of space in which we situate and order all concrete spatial units and all objects of the external world is not itself to be discovered anywhere *in* this external world. Therefore, the general idea of space must already be present in our minds *a priori*.

Like the idea of space, Kant considers the idea of time to be something that is already integrated into our cognitive apparatus, prior to and independently of any concrete sense-perception. It is only on condition of our possessing this inherent idea of time that we are able to fit events into a temporal sequence of 'before', 'after' etc.

Time is a necessary representation that grounds all intuitions [...]. [24]

And just as we can never shake off that part of our mental faculty which ensures that our ideas of things are always ideas of *things in space*, so too are we compelled by our own mental make-up to embed all sense-impressions in a context of *events in time*. It is impossible, Kant says, for us to register, even for a single day, our sense-impressions 'timelessly', i.e. in a manner that would not involve organizing them in terms of temporal succession:

[...] all objects of the senses [...] are in time, and necessarily stand in relations of time. [25]

This passage of Kant's first *Critique* also includes a brief remark that casts light on a key further element of his philosophy. He points out that human beings remain 'captives' of these two 'forms of intuition', space and time, our whole lives long. In other words, we can never perceive objects as they really are *in themselves*, but rather always only as we know and receive them through the grid of our spatio-temporal sense-perception. Kant formulates this as follows:

What may be the case with objects in themselves and abstracted from all this receptivity of our sensibility remains entirely unknown to us. [26]

What Kant calls here the 'object in itself' he refers to later as 'the thing-in-itself'. This 'thing-in-itself , then – i.e. an object as it is outside of the perceptual grid which makes it an object *for us* – remains hidden from us forever. The objects we get to perceive are always objects which we have ordered in terms of space and time:

> We are acquainted with nothing except our way of perceiving them, which is peculiar to us, and which therefore does not necessarily pertain to every being, though to be sure it pertains to every human being. [27]

Other beings, such as bees, perhaps see things quite differently. They see a significantly broader range of colours than human beings, have a far finer perception of metallic shades and can, for example, make out with their eyes whether nectar is present on the pistil of a flower. But even bees see a flower only as their *a priori* 'forms of intuition' allow them to. The flower 'in itself' remains as hidden from their perception as it does from that of human beings.

But this, in the end, is irrelevant to the question of *human* knowledge. Since all human beings, all over the world, share the same cognitive apparatus with the same *a priori* 'forms of intuition', we also all share a single perspective on things and arrive at similar results. To this important chapter of the *Critique of Pure Reason* dealing with space and time Kant gave the title: *'Transcendental Aesthetic'*. 'Aesthetic' here draws on the meaning of the term in Greek, where it signified simply: 'perception'. The chapter is so called because it deals with the conditions of possibility of all sense-perception. Its result is very clear: if our physical senses turn stimuli into actual perceptions, this is only possible thanks to our *a priori* mental faculty of ordering these stimuli in terms of space and time. It is only due to this *a priori* grid that we are able to perceive 'raw sense-impressions' as things displaying defined and specific spatial and temporal sequences and structures.

The Categories

In the following chapter things become even more interesting. Kant entitles this chapter *'Transcendental Logic'*, from the Greek word *logos*, meaning 'reason', 'understanding', or 'thinking', because it deals with how it is possible for the mind to *logically* process those sense-impressions which have already been ordered in terms of space and time. Now there comes into play that part of the human thought-apparatus that Kant calls 'the understanding'. Until this point it had been a matter only of sense-perception which basically operates automatically, since everything that is perceived is pressed, without any real need for conscious intervention, into a spatio-temporal grid.

But now Kant poses the question of what then happens with these 'raw' but spatio-temporally ordered sense-data. The cognitive apparatus proper now springs into action, for it is its job to 'work up', in the blink of an eye, this entire raw material of spatio-temporally ordered sense-impressions and to make judgments about reality on its basis. At this point, the senses have already done their work and lend no aid to the understanding in its specific work of making judgments:

> Thus it is correctly said that the senses do not err; yet not because they always judge correctly, but because they do not judge at all. [28]

'The senses do not judge at all': by this Kant means that they provide only the 'raw material': a jangling noise; then a specific scent; and fractions of a second later a blinding light and birdsong. If judgments about reality are made on the basis of this 'raw material', it is the understanding alone that does this. It alone can and must judge whether, when a jangling noise is perceived, it is a case of a rattlesnake approaching, a bunch of keys being shaken, or an alarm-clock going off:

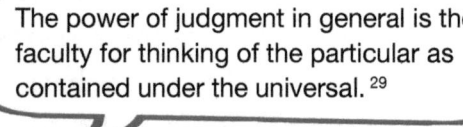

> The power of judgment in general is the faculty for thinking of the particular as contained under the universal. [29]

In our example the 'particular' – the loud jangling – might initially be thought of as 'contained under' the 'universal': 'threatening gestures of rattlesnakes' (since this species can indeed create jangling noises with its tail); or as 'contained under' the 'universal': 'sounds arising when metal strikes against metal', as in the case of a shaken bunch of keys. The understanding, then, might also make the judgment that the reality confronting us here is a rattlesnake or a bunch of keys. At the very latest, however, once we have opened our eyes and seen the specific shape of the clock, the numbers on its dial and the clock-hand, our understanding will succeed in assigning the perceived 'particular' to its proper place under the 'universal': 'alarm-clock'.

But how, precisely, are such assignings of 'particulars' to their places under 'universals' – such exercises of 'the power of judgment' in the sense in which Kant uses this term – carried out within the human mind? What does it really mean to 'think'? Kant, we have seen, defined the activity of our understanding as a 'comparing, connecting and separating' of sense-impressions. But how does the understanding succeed in grasping, comparing, connecting and separating, in so short a time, the chaos represented by so many sense-impressions? How do we actually arrive at a 'judgment' in the sense in which Kant uses this term? Kant's answer is succinct and incisive: with the aid of the categories. Each human being has at his disposal exactly twelve different cognitive categories, by means of which he orders, with lightning speed, the whole chaos of crowding sense-impressions and comes to four different kinds of judgment:

> If we abstract from all content of a judgment in general and attend only to the mere form of the understanding in it, we find that the function of thinking in that can be brought under four titles, each of which contains under itself three moments. They can suitably be represented in the following table. [30]

The famous table of four types of judgment and twelve categories formulated by Kant is a milestone in the theory of knowledge and is still a subject of discussion and debate today. Kant takes over parts of this table from Aristotle and thereby continues the long tradition, stretching back to antiquity, of presenting in a list or diagram all the logical possibilities open to human thought. He painstakingly sets out, under the four broader headings: 'Judgments of Quantity'. 'Of Quality', 'Of Relation' and 'Of Modality', all the twelve possible cognitive categories:

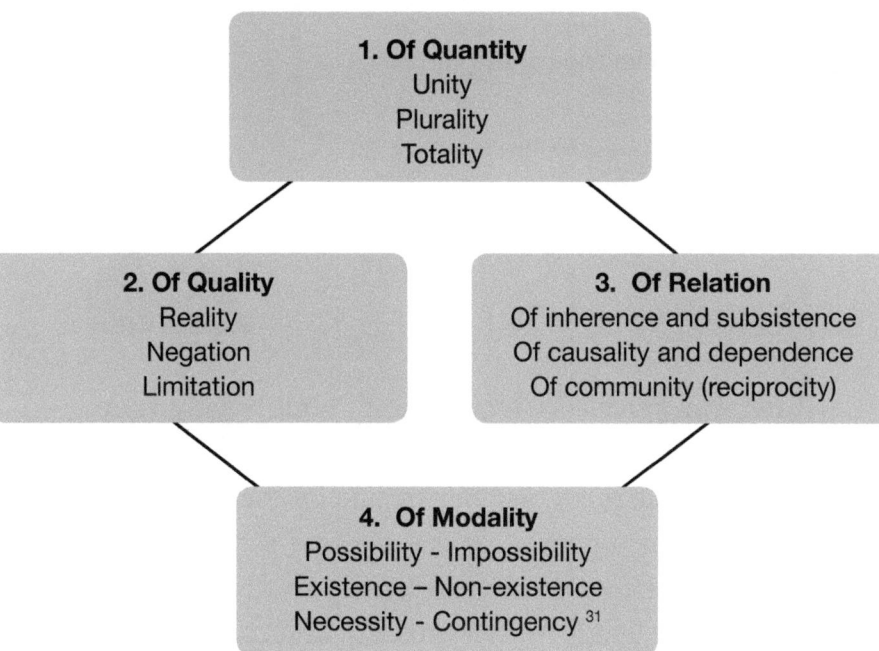

1. Of Quantity
Unity
Plurality
Totality

2. Of Quality
Reality
Negation
Limitation

3. Of Relation
Of inherence and subsistence
Of causality and dependence
Of community (reciprocity)

4. Of Modality
Possibility - Impossibility
Existence – Non-existence
Necessity - Contingency [31]

Kant believed that he had succeeded, with this table, in comprehensively identifying all the categories and forms of judgment that we human beings use, every day, to think. These twelve categories, then, and the corresponding four 'forms of judgment', are the decisive (indeed the only) tools by means of which our thought-apparatus carves exact knowledge out of the chaotic mass of 'raw sense-impressions'.

> This is the listing of all original pure concepts of synthesis that the understanding contains in itself a priori [...]. [32]

The term 'synthesis' which Kant employs here is derived from the Greek for 'putting together'. And this is indeed the main task performed by the categories: the 'putting together' of the various sense-impressions under overarching concepts, so that they can be contemplated in their entirety and combination. The understanding, then, uses the categories to create a kind of 'panorama' of all sense-impressions and thereby to arrive at judgments about reality.

These remarks suffice, in fact, basically to describe the whole process of human 'knowing' as Kant understood it. But Kant also points out in a later section of his main work – a section which he entitles 'Tran-

scendental Deduction' – that there must, of course, be constantly involved in this whole process of human 'knowing' a thinking subject who generates these acts of knowledge. And this *thinking subject* – i.e. the perceiving and cogitating human being – not only organizes sense-impressions with the help of the categories but also constantly refers all these thought-processes back to himself as *his* thought-processes.

The 'I think' must be able to accompany all my representations. [33]

All my sense-impressions, and all the judgments which result from the drawing of these sense-impressions under the categories, are referred, even as they arise, automatically to this 'I think' – or, in other words, referred to *me* and to my own self-awareness.

> For the manifold representations that are given in a certain intuition would not, all together, be my representations if they did not, all together, belong to a self-consciousness [...]. [34]

In summary: Every act of knowledge takes place in two stages. First, 'raw sense-impressions' – i.e. sounds, smells, tastes, and visual images – are perceived through application of the *a priori* spatio-temporal grid and thereby ordered into spatial relations and temporal sequences of 'here and there', 'before and after'; then, in a second step, these 'raw' (but already spatio-temporally ordered) sense-impressions are used, with the help of the categories, as the basis for judgments – i.e. are subsumed under more general concepts by being 'compared, connected and separated' with and from one another; and all the while all these thought-events are, even as they arise, automatically related back to 'me' as the subject thinking them.

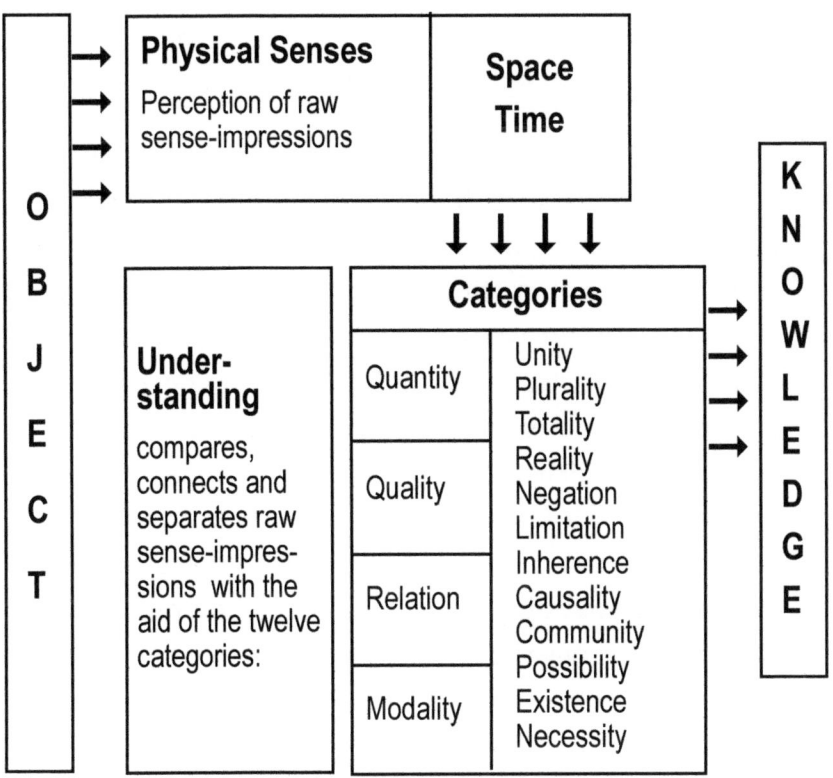

The Categories on the Motorway

The actual functions of the categories in our thinking apparatus are, at first, hard to understand. Kant himself gives no example of this. He excuses this omission by saying that, since his book was already very bulky, he did not want to make it still bulkier with examples. But this decision has been the despair of whole generations of philosophy students attempting to fathom just what concrete significance the categories have for knowledge. Because there do indeed arise such questions as: how exactly do these twelve rather stiff-sounding categories – unity; plurality, totality; reality; negation; limitation; inherence; causality; community; possibility/impossibility; existence/non-existence; necessity/contingency – help me to arrive at judgments and knowledge? What exactly is meant by these four 'forms of judgment' – quantity, quality, relation, and modality – which Kant claims them to fall under in their turn; and how exactly does the process Kant calls 'synthesis' work?

The use of the categories is, if Kant is right, a necessary and permanent component part of our cognitive faculty and must, therefore, function reliably, and as if as a matter of course, in our daily lives. Let us, then, illustrate this everyday use of the categories by the example of a common experience. Imagine the following situation: we are driving on the motorway, in the left-hand lane, at high speed. Suddenly, we see an object lying in the road, reddish-brown and about 15 inches long but indistinct in shape. We are alarmed and a thousand thoughts shoot through our head. What can it be? Is it dangerous? What *quality, quantity, relation* and *modality* does it have? How should we react? Our understanding works flat out to quickly answer these questions. In a split second we apply all our twelve categories to this object, so as to judge of its nature and react accordingly.

Unity: This thing, considered as a single thing (a 'unit'), belongs to the class 'reddish-brown objects'.

Plurality: Many (a plurality of) logs and wooden cases are brownish-red, as are many bricks. It could be a log or a brick.

Totality: All (the totality of) logs are heavy and bulky, as are all bricks!

→   **First judgment:** The thing in question is significant and dangerous from the point of view of **quantity**.

Reality: The thing in the road measures approximately 15 x 8 inches.

Negation: The thing in the road cannot simply be smoothly driven over.

Limitation: The thing in the road does not belong there.

→ **Second judgment:** The thing has the **quality** of a serious obstacle.

Inherence and Subsistence: It is inherent in the heavy substance of this thing that it will shatter windscreens.

Causality and Dependence: If we do not brake or swerve right now, this brick or log shall be the cause of a possibly fatal effect on our car and ourselves.

Community and Reciprocity: The speed we are driving at and the heaviness of the thing in the road shall combine, 'in common', to produce an even more severe impact.

→ **Third judgment:** Relation – that is to say, relation between this thing in the road and our car and ourselves – is present here in a high degree, and has certain effects upon us.

Possibility – Impossibility: It is possible that the object will be thrown into the air and hit us or that it will be thrown into the air and not hit us. But it is not to be excluded as impossible that it will hit us.

Existence – Non-Existence: There is no doubt that this thing exists and is there; it is barring our way.

Necessity - Contingency: It is necessary to react to the obstacle in some way: to brake or to change lanes and not to leave things to chance.

→ **Fourth judgment:** The **modalities** are such that we cannot rely just on chance and good luck.

We recognize ever more clearly that we need either to brake to a halt or swerve. But right behind and next to us many other cars are also driving at high speed. While we hesitate as to whether to apply the brake, the thing in the road looms rapidly nearer. And look! Suddenly it moves from left to right. In rapid mental reaction, we once again (and still in the space of a split second) pass four of the twelve categories over the object in the road and 'work up' the resulting individual judgments, with equally lightning speed, into a tentative new knowledge of reality.

Unity: Considered as a single thing (a 'unit'), this 15-inch-long thing now belongs to the class 'reddish-brown objects which move from left to right'.

Plurality: Many (a plurality of) small animals are reddish-brown. Many small animals can move. Many rabbits, squirrels and foxes are reddish-brown.

Totality: All animals have bodies.

Causality: If this rabbit, squirrel or fox manages to cross the motorway lane in time, we will not have to apply the brakes.

So it is an animal, then! We squint our eyes, ease the pressure of our foot on the gas pedal, and hope that the creature succeeds in getting off the road in time. But something is not right. As we run this thing through the categories, 'error messages' keep popping up. All rabbits have a scampering gait; all foxes and squirrels lope or spring and have a clearly noticeable tail. But the animal in the road is of roughly square shape, does not scamper, lope or spring, and has no tail. It is as if we are jinxed here: the thing in the road just can't be made to fit the typical characteristics. We recall Kant's words:

To compare something as a characteristic mark with a thing is to judge. The thing itself is the subject; the characteristic mark is the predicate. [35]

The thing on the road, then, is the subject, while 'scampering' is the predicate (or the 'characteristic mark'). But the thing in question does not scamper; it does not move like any sort of animal moves. The 'characteristic marks', or 'predicates', that I want to ascribe to this 'subject' do not in fact accord with it at all. Is our judgment wrong, then? While we hectically set about rethinking this judgment, the thing suddenly rises up off the road and begins to fly back and forth in the air. In a state of high tension, we apply our categories for a third and last time to this sense-perception (under the latest, new form it has assumed).

Unity: Considered as a single thing (a 'unit'), this thing now belongs to the class: 'reddish-brown objects which are roughly square, move from left to right, and fly back and forth in the air'.

Plurality: Many (a plurality of) birds are reddish-brown. Many paper bags are also reddish-brown.

Totality: All birds can rise, to some extent, into the air. All paper bags can be blown into the air by the wind.

Reality: The flying thing is 15 inches in length and squarish.

Negation: No bird is 15 inches in length and squarish. The thing on the road is not a bird.

Limitation: The paper bag does not belong on the motorway.

Causality: If a paper bag is caught by the wind, this can be the cause of its flying back and forth in the air as the wind-direction changes.

Inherence and Subsistence: It is inherent in the nature of a paper bag that its substance contains very little mass and that, due to its lightness, it can be blown into the air.

Possibility - Impossibility: It is possible that the

bag might get hooked onto the front of the car and pressed onto the windscreen, and that it might, for a moment, block our view of the road. But it is impossible that a paper bag might shatter the windscreen.

Necessity - Contingency: There is no necessity that we swerve or brake to a halt. It is unlikely that the bag will get hooked onto the front of the car. But should the contingency arise that it does get caught on the windscreen and block our view, we can, if necessary, activate our windscreen-wipers.

What a marvellously reassuring piece of knowledge we have arrived at. The object is just a paper bag that is now dancing harmlessly in the air! So let us sum up: By repeated application of the categories we have arrived, in fractions of seconds, at three different working knowledges of the reality confronting us. First we judged the object to be a log, wooden box, or brick; then to be a running animal; and finally to be a harmless paper bag. Our twelve categories, then, finally enable us to breathe a sigh of relief. They have not let us down, even in such a stressful situation.

But what exactly are 'categories'? In what, precisely, do these peculiar instruments of the understanding consist and, above all – where do they come from? How did they arise? Did the human beings of the

Stone Age already work, in their thinking, with these twelve categories? Or have they taken form only in the course of human evolution?

Kant was a philosopher of exemplary thoroughness who thought everything through to the end and he showed himself ready to confront also this question. But surprisingly, in the passage where he does, he concedes that even he is not in a position to give an exact definition of these categories and can say nothing about their origin or possible process of emergence:

I deliberately spare myself the definitions of these categories in this treatise, although I should like to be in possession of (these definitions). [36]

But even if we do not know just where the categories come from, we still know with absolute certainty (if we follow Kant) that there are, and must be, such categories. Because without them we would never be able to order and organize the 'raw material' of the many smells, sounds and sights that make up our day-to-day harvest of sense-perceptions and 'work up' this raw material into judgments and knowledge about reality. Considered from the point of view of transcendental philosophy, then, the categories are necessary concepts of the understanding – that is to say, pure instruments of the human thinking apparatus – which are indispensable if we are to be capable of imposing logical sense and conceptual coherence upon the many thousands of sense-perceptions that crowd in on us every waking second of every day:

All sensible intuitions stand under the categories, as conditions under which alone their manifold can come together in one consciousness. [37]

Kant speaks of the categories as 'pure concepts of the understanding' inasmuch as these categories must be inherently present in us prior to all empirical experience. Causality, for example, like the other eleven categories, is nothing that can be recognized to exist inherently *in* any object that is perceived by us through our senses. Rather, relations of cause and effect come to be 'stamped', as it were, upon the impressions ('intuitions') of our senses only when the understanding goes into action upon these latter. Thus, we see the paper bag flying about in the air and we hear the wind whistling. But that the bag is flying about *because* of the wind – i.e. that these two elements of our perception: 'wind' and 'flying bag' stand in a relation of *cause and effect* – this is a piece of knowledge that is provided by our understanding alone, which lays, as it were, the category 'causality' over both of these sense-perceptions and thereby connects them up to one another.

Knowledge as the Interplay of Sense-Perception and Thought

The reason why Kant considers it to be so important to establish that the categories constitute 'pure concepts of the understanding' is because he also explains thereby the possibility of all the theories proposed by the science of physics. Physicists, Kant contends, do nothing other than take the abstract *a priori* categories which inhere in our understanding and use these in order to form complex theories. By engaging in reflections involving the faculty of the understanding alone, they arrive at propositions which enrich our knowledge of reality.

But is such a thing really possible? Can there really be valid 'synthetic *a priori* judgments' – i.e. judgments which are arrived at in abstraction from, or prior to, any sense-impression-based experience? To this question Kant initially answers 'yes'. Because physicists are indeed able, making use of nothing besides the pure categories of the understanding, to set up scientific theories and 'thought experiments' which these same physicists go on only *later* to apply to the real natural world and to test out by means of measurements and literal experiments involving more than just thoughts. The category of causality in particular plays a prominent role here, since this category is often used as a hypothesis in the establishment and investigation of natural laws. In their research into Nature and its laws, physicists almost always look for relations of cause and effect. But this notion of causality is initially present simply in the head of the physicist; it is read into Nature only afterward.

Take the case of a physicist who sets out to investigate whether, where heat remains constant, differently-constituted objects melt at different rates. He may proceed as follows: he first formulates, making use only of the abstract categories of substance, causality and reciprocity, a logical law which sets up the expectation that objects with a soft organic structure may possibly melt faster than very dense objects with a firmer non-organic structure. This assumedly applying physical law, then, is one which he acquires, initially, by drawing on the *a priori* categories of logic alone. Only after having so acquired it does he proceed to heat up, for example, vegetable fat, beeswax, tin, and iron in order to test his hypothetical 'law of Nature', and finds his hypothesis that denser materials will tend to take longer to melt to be indeed confirmed.

Mankind, then, is always, in the first instance, the lawgiver for Nature and Mankind's examination of events in Nature is an examination of these natural events on Mankind's own terms. Hence Kant's provocative formulation: 'our knowledge must not conform to objects; rather, objects must conform to our knowledge'. Kant compares in this regard his discovery of the 'categorial' activity of our thinking apparatus, by virtue of which we make judgments on Nature and its objects according to logical laws, to the 'Copernican turn' in astronomy:

This would be just like the first thoughts of Copernicus who, when he did not make good progress in the explanation of the celestial

motions if he assumed that the entire celestial host revolves around the observer, tried to see if he might not have greater success if he made the observer revolve and left the stars at rest. [38]

Just as Copernicus was obliged to recognize that due to the prejudice that Man stayed motionless at the centre of the universe all judgments about the motions of the stars had been, for centuries, false, we too need to recognize that we repeatedly impose upon reality ideas which do not necessarily really correspond to this latter.

Regardless of whether we are physicists or scientific laymen, it must constantly be clear to us that it is we ourselves who, with the aid of the categories, first set up a theory and only then apply it – be it to the planets or to some other aspect of Nature – and test it against sense-perceptions.

In this light, it is clear that a large part of the work of arriving at true knowledge is performed by the human mind and its *a priori* equipment. Every theory, however – and this is the demand that Kant places on science – must also be supported by empirical sense-perceptions if the knowledge it yields is indeed to be true knowledge. One can, indeed, with the aid of the categories, set up logically well thought-out hypotheses; but one must be able also to point to real 'intuitions' which confirm these. 'Synthetic *a priori* judgments' – i.e. insights and laws which have been artificially derived from the pure categories of the understanding alone – are possible, indeed, but do not yet amount to sure and established knowledge about reality.

For Kant, knowledge consists always in the co-dependent interplay of sense-perception and understanding. If we had only sense-impressions, we would drown in the chaos of an infinite mass of perceptual stimuli; but if we had only the ordering and synthesizing understanding and its categories, we would get lost in abstract speculation:

> For it is not to be forgotten that all knowledge has two ends by which it can be caught, an a priori end and one which is a posteriori. [39]

What applies to physics also applies to mathematics. Thanks to those 'a priori forms of intuition' that are space and time the mathematician can come up with a whole series of 'synthetic *a priori* judgments'. It requires, for example, nothing else besides that faculty of necessarily spatial representation which Kant holds to be *a priori* present in all human minds to ground the proposition: 'a straight line is the short-est distance between two points'. But such geometri-cal 'synthetic *a priori* judgments' are not real knowl-edge either. Kant held such geometrical propositions – as, indeed, he did all mathematical propositions – to be only *formally* correct and to hold true only on the *formal* level:

> Whether there can be things that must be intuited in this form is still left unsettled. Consequently, all mathematical concepts are not, by themselves, cognitions [...]. [40]

Just because it is possible to arrive by mathematical calculation at the notion of a sphere as an ideal geo-metrical solid, this does not mean that there really exists in Nature a physical body which corresponds to this ideal solid – i.e. that there really "can be things that must be intuited in this form". There belongs to all true knowledge not only an *a priori* judgment of the understanding but also, always, a sense-percep-tion (an 'intuition').

In the third great section of the *Critique of Pure Reason* – the 'Transcendental Dialectic' – Kant describes the so-called 'antinomies of pure reason', which are indeed nothing other than the insoluble self-contradictions in which human reason becomes entangled when it attempts to force through its claims to true knowledge *without* regard to real sense-perceptions:

Thus, pure reason [...] contains nothing but regulative principles which, [...] if one misunderstands them and takes

them to be constitutive principles of transcendent cognition, [...] produce a dazzling but deceptive delusion [...] and thus also eternal contradictions and controversies. [41]

Due to these 'contradictions and controversies' reason is obliged, finally, to acknowledge its own limits.

It is humiliating for human reason that it accomplishes nothing in its pure use [...]. [42]

The 'pure use' of reason (i.e. its use without recourse to sense-experience of any kind), such as is found, for example, in theology's attempts to provide 'rational proofs of God's existence', leads not to knowledge but only to speculation and is – Kant leaves his readers in no doubt – completely worthless:

Now, I assert that all attempts of a merely speculative use of reason in regard to theology are entirely fruitless and by their internal constitution null and nugatory. [43]

Kant hereby arrived, at the end of the *Critique of Pure Reason*, at a result which many found hard to swallow. He became the first philosopher in Western history to prove that 'God' was a topic about which human beings, given the structure of the human faculty of knowledge, were incapable of really *knowing* anything at all.

God is Not an Object of Knowledge

God is not an object of sense-perception; no one has ever seen Him. Therefore – since, as we have seen, reason is always partially reliant on sense-perception in order to arrive at true knowledge – it is beyond reason's capacities to *know* either that there *is* a God or that there is *not*. God's existence cannot be experienced and therefore cannot be proven. Somewhat to Kant's discomfort, he had to recognize that the church had, for centuries, been founded on an implicit denial of this truth. The Christian church still requires of its believers that they love God as one loves a real existing being. Kant considers this to be an irrational, excessive demand made on Christian believers:

> But love for God as inclination is impossible, for He is not an object of the senses. The same thing toward human beings is indeed possible but cannot be commanded, for it is not within the power of any human being to love someone merely on command. [44]

As a rational thinker Kant was unwilling to join in any prayers that alluded to 'immaculate conception' and other such ideas, which were irrational inasmuch as they lacked both confirming sense-perception and comprehensible internal logic. For this reason he stubbornly avoided attending church services and agreed, even in his official capacity as university rector, only on rare occasions to visit Königsberg's churches. He had, indeed, a very sceptical view of all religious rituals:

In religion in general, submission, adoration with bowed head, and remorseful and anxious gestures and voice seem to be the only appropriate conduct in the presence of the deity and so to have been adopted and still preserved by most peoples [...]. [45]

One feels clearly here Kant's commitment to the spirit of the Enlightenment, which he elsewhere defined as Man's 'emergence from his self-incurred minority'. His wish was for a society of upright citizens who would subject everything to rational criticism. The result arrived at by the *Critique of Pure Reason* leaves no doubt here as regards religion. Since every rational knowledge-claim is reliant on the interplay between sense-perception on the one hand and the *a priori* categories of the understanding on the other, one cannot claim to really *know* anything of either God or the immortality of the soul or the nature of good and evil.

These results of Kant's, however, not only deprive theology of the status of a science but philosophy as well, at least insofar as philosophy deals with metaphysical topics. Kant would appear, then, to have to terminate at this point his own philosophical project. But, astonishingly, he manages to avoid this, namely as follows: It is, he argues, in the very nature of Man to have to pose questions which cannot be answered by human reason:

Human reason has the peculiar fate [...] that it is burdened with questions which it cannot dismiss, since they are given to it as problems by the nature of reason itself, but which it also cannot answer, since they transcend every capacity of human reason. [46]

Among such questions are not only those about God and life after death but, above all, those about the true nature of justice or the freedom of the human will. Does Man have free will? Are there such things as 'just laws'? Is there such a thing as 'moral action' and, if so, what does it consist in? It follows, indeed, from Kant's 'critique of knowledge' that there can be no really reliable answer to these questions either. 'Justice', 'morality', 'good and evil' are not possible objects of *scientific* knowledge since they cannot be perceived through the senses; 'justice' is nothing that can be seen or smelt or tasted; in the absence of all sense-perception it can be the object only of *theoretical* reason, so no real *knowledge* of it can result.

And yet, Kant goes on to argue, every society is obliged to give to these *theoretically* insoluble questions some sort of *practical* answer. Thus, these 'unanswerable' questions are always answered, one way or the other, after all. Since earliest times there have always been taboos, rules, customs, traditions and laws and legislation has direct practical consequences for the citizen of any state. However, now Kant takes an unexpected but vital further step. After proving, over the thousand and more pages of the *Critique of Pure Reason*, that human reason is unable to know anything of invisible ideas and ideals, he now states that human beings must concern themselves with such questions all the same. Human beings are compelled to seek moral and ethical orientation for their actions, even if reason – and Kant never retreats from this position even in his work on morality and ethics – can provide us with no certain knowledge in such fields.

'What Ought I To Do?'
The Critique of Practical Reason

This is why Kant calls his second great work the *Critique of Practical Reason*. Here, he investigates whether one can establish practical principles necessary for, and beneficial to, human coexistence even if the theory of knowledge cannot prove these principles. Kant thus draws a distinction here between *theoretical and practical reason*. Reason has two aspects or, to put it differently, two functions: a cognitive-theoretical one and a practical-ethical one. Theoretical reason seeks always only sure and certain knowledge; but practical reason has the task of establishing moral principles, indeed moral laws, which, even if they are not provable, can lay claim to absolute validity.

Kant considers, then, the realm of practical reason to comprise all that must be thought to be a necessary truth even if it is located beyond the limits of the competence of pure reason. Already, indeed, in the *Critique of Pure Reason* Kant prepares for this later foray into the realm of practical reason. He draws there a terminological distinction which he maintains through all the rest of his work. Where he focuses on those regular activities of the human thought-apparatus which lead to sure knowledge (i.e. the use of the categories, 'synthesis', and finally the making of judgments) he will often speak not of the faculty of reason but specifically of the faculty of *understanding (Verstand)*. But where he addresses activities of this apparatus which go beyond this and which concern principles that can only be thought (not experienced) Kant uses the term 'reason' *(Vernunft)* in a sense quite separate and distinct from 'understanding':

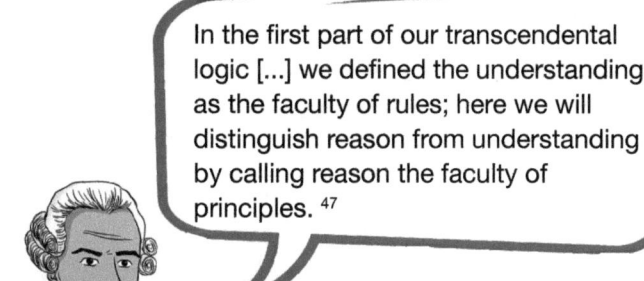

In the first part of our transcendental logic [...] we defined the understanding as the faculty of rules; here we will distinguish reason from understanding by calling reason the faculty of principles. [47]

Practical reason, then, must reach out beyond the activity of 'pure reason' in the narrower sense – i.e. the 'working-up' of concepts and making of judgments via the categories – and concern itself with final principles. What Kant is aiming at here is an ethical principle binding on all which would tell us how to act rightly in our lives. But is this even possible? Surely one needs different action-strategies in different situations? Can there really be a single principle that is valid for everyone at every point in time and equally applicable everywhere?

Kant's answer to this question is a clear 'yes!' In his two major works on ethics, the *Critique of Practical Reason* and the *Groundwork of the Metaphysics of Morals*, he does indeed develop an ethical concept which is applicable beyond all concrete situations and experiences: a universal principle for right action which has become world famous under the name 'categorical imperative'. Kant's own concise and brilliant formulation of it runs:

So act that the maxim of your will could always hold at the same time as a principle in a giving of universal law. [48]

By 'maxim' here Kant means the individual principle by which each of us orients our own actions. The categorical imperative, then, runs (expressed in more modern language): 'so act that the principle by which you orient your actions could also at any time be the principle orienting the actions of all other human beings' or (put still more simply) 'so act that your actions might become a model for everyone's actions everywhere'.

With this categorical imperative, Kant claimed, he had created a universally binding principle of moral orientation. Any individual can apply it in any situation, at any time, at any place. Whatever moral problem he faces, he can deal with it by applying this principle. He need only ask himself whether he would wish all individuals to act in the same way as he is contemplating acting. The categorical imperative is thereby globally valid and universally applicable. But Kant does not rest content with this:

A metaphysics of morals is therefore indispensably necessary [...], because morals themselves remain subject to

all sorts of corruption as long as we are without that clue and supreme norm by which to appraise them correctly. [49]

Kant searches, then, for such a 'clue and supreme norm' with the aid of which all existing morals and doctrines of morality can be evaluated. The aim he sets himself here is very high. It seems even to be arrogant, given that philosophers have been puzzling since antiquity over this question. Is, then, Kant's categorical imperative really superior to all other ethical principles? And, if so, why is this the case?

In order to answer this question let us set out, with Kant, on the adventure of a short philosophical detective story. There have been, and still are, basically only four general ethical conceptions which prescribe morally good and right ways of life for Man. We all know these conceptions, even if we are not aware of it, because they do indeed form the maxims of our day-to-day action. They are: the hedonistic maxim; the utilitarian; the *eudaemonic*; and the legalistic. Kant described and criticized all four of these maxims in turn and proposed at the end, in their stead, his own ethical maxim, a fifth and morally highest.

The Critique of Hedonism: The Pleasure Principle Knows No Morality

One of the oldest general orientations for human action is so-called 'hedonism', named after the Greek *hedone*, which means 'pleasure'. Hedonism, then, is the doctrine of the primacy of pleasure. A 'hedonistic imperative' would run: 'so act that your actions gain you the maximum possible pleasure and spare you, so far as is possible, unpleasure.'

This philosophical tradition is very old, reaching back to Epicurus. Epicurus argued that humans, as sensual beings, have certain basic needs – for eating and drinking, sexuality, sociability, recreation etc. – which we not only must, but indeed *should*, regularly satisfy, our whole lives long. A person's sense for what gives him pleasure helps him to make sound, good decisions. By seeking always to maximize pleasure and avoid unpleasure, a person wards off harm and leads a sensually fulfilled and happy life. And indeed even today, two and a half thousand years after Epicurus, we live according to this 'pleasure principle' in many areas of our lives. It is not only when choosing a boyfriend or girlfriend, a holiday destination, or a meal in a restaurant that we let ourselves to be swayed by pleasurable 'feeling'. Which seminars, theatre plays, or film-shows we attend also depends on 'whether we feel like it'. Such 'hedonistic' motives can often even influence our choice of what job we train for or what subject we study, indeed what politics we support: while some people enjoy party-political work and the prospect of power and responsibility, others take no part in political organizations just because they 'don't feel like' getting involved in such things. 'Feeling', then, in the sense of anticipated pleasure, is surely a life-counsellor accepted by many. But is it a good counsellor? Ought one really always seek to maximize pleasure and avoid unpleasure?

Kant finds that hedonism fails as an ethical principle and as a maxim for action already for the simple reason that orienting one's action by the pleasure principle may lead, in the cases of ten different people, to ten different results. This is because 'maximizing pleasure' means something different for each individual, and each will 'feel like' performing this action or that one, depending on taste. So if we accept that 'right action' can be defined as just the act that one 'feels like' doing, each one of a group of people, though all acting differently in the same situation, will be able to claim their action to have been the morally right and correct one. But in Kant's view a moral law fit to guide us in our practice of life must be objectively valid for all, i.e. be capable of being applied similarly by all. Already just for this reason Kant considers hedonism to be unviable as an ethical principle for human society:

[...] a principle that is based only on the subjective condition of receptivity to a pleasure or displeasure (which can always be cognized only

empirically and cannot be valid in the same way for all rational beings) [...] can never furnish a practical law. [50]

A second, equally great drawback of any maxim of action oriented by pleasure consists in the fact that achieving one's own pleasure can result in unpleasure for someone else. But since Kant defines an ethical principle as a principle that must be simultaneously and equally binding on all, the 'pleasure principle' proves self-contradictory. Thus, a sadistic dictator who takes pleasure in torturing his subjects acts, according to the hedonistic maxim, subjectively rightly, since such torture increases his own pleasure; objectively, however, his acting in this way creates unpleasure, and even pain and suffering, for others. Kant considers pleasure – or, as he often puts it, 'inclination' – to be, quite generally, no good counsellor in moral matters. For even the case of a benign dictator – one who is 'favourably inclined' toward his subjects and rules over them, because of this inclination, in 'moral' manner – would not, for Kant, satisfy the demands of true morality:

In a word, the moral law demands obedience from duty, not from a (mere) predilection [...]. [51]

The hedonistic approach is indeed highly questionable as an ethical principle because pleasure is often insufficient as a means of determining what is morally good. Already Plato had used a simple example to critique hedonism: if someone feels a strong urge to scratch an itch, the scratching may indeed be very pleasurable; but this does not mean that either the scratching or the itch possess any high moral quality.

The Critique of Utilitarianism: Weighing Up 'Benefit' is Dangerous

The second ethical principle is 'utilitarianism', named from the Latin word *utilitas*, which means 'usefulness' or 'benefit'. It is the contention of this line of ethical thought that people should orient their actions in terms of just these latter considerations. A 'utilitarian imperative' would run: 'so act that you gain through your actions the maximum possible benefit'.

This imperative too is one that has achieved widespread acceptance in our society. We do in fact constantly weigh up, every day, whether we will gain greater benefit by riding to work on the train or on our bicycle; by investing in a pair of expensive but hard-wearing shoes or by buying a cheap pair that will soon wear out; by buying a car or renting one; by marrying or by staying single; by claiming a tax rebate on our bedroom, saying we use it for work, or by being honest and declaring it as just a bedroom; by buying a ticket on the subway train or by trying to dodge the fare. Likely costs and benefits of our actions are always being assessed: what is it likely to cost me if I am caught fare-dodging, and what will it cost me to buy a ticket? There is almost no end to the number of such 'utilitarian' decisions that are made daily especially in capitalist societies. Calculations of benefit are omnipresent. Even in democratic elections most voters will tend to opt for the party from whom they expect to receive the greatest possible economic benefit.

The drawback of this second maxim for the orientation of action is as clear as was that of the first: Something that is to someone's benefit need not thereby, automatically, be something morally good. It brings 'benefit', indeed, of a sort, to ride the train from one station to the next without giving oneself the expense of a ticket; but 'morally good' such an action most definitely is not, since the 'benefit' that the individual fare-dodger thereby acquires is a 'cost' and a definite harm to the community at large. In other words, what is a benefit to one person can be an injury to another. 'Utilitarianism', then, appears *prima facie* to be a very egotistical form of ethics, if one can call it an 'ethics' at all.

But already in the period – the 18th Century – when this utilitarian idea was first being formulated in systematic form, its proponents were aware of this weak point in their doctrine. For this reason, their formulations propose that the action which should be considered a morally good action is an action which maximizes not the benefit of the *individual* but rather the benefit of the *greatest possible number of the members of society as a whole*. It was the British philosophers Hutcheson and Mill who first propounded the systematic utilitarian argument that all social and political action should aim to bring about the happiness and the benefit of the greatest possible number of people. Since Hutcheson and Mill the utilitarian imperative has run, then, rather as follows: 'so act that your actions lead to the maximum possible benefit for the maximum possible number of those who are affected by them'.

Such an expanded utilitarian imperative dictates, for example, that when a politician plans the building of a new subway station, his plan should not place this station in front of his own house, so as to ensure quicker journeys for himself alone, but rather at whatever place will be to the greatest benefit of the greatest number of citizens. He cannot, of course, make every citizen happy since, wherever he places it, there will always remain a minority who will have to walk further to reach the station than most others. But it is the view of utilitarians that this is not only justifiable but, in many cases, absolutely necessary. When building ill-smelling sewage or waste incineration plants or noisy airports, it must be morally right, they argue, to push ahead with this vital infrastructure even against the protests of a negatively affected minority, since it is surely to the benefit of the population as a whole. Precisely in the sphere of political decisions, then, utilitarianism, with its aim of achieving the greatest benefit for the greatest number, appears to be the best of all moral principles.

But Kant does not see things this way. It is utilitarianism in its very core that he is criticizing when he proposes that, above all considerations of use or benefit, each human being needs necessarily to be considered as an end in himself. That is to say: one must never try to raise to the status of a moral principle the notion that a minority can simply be passed over with a view to achieving some greater benefit for the majority:

Now I say that the human being, and in general every rational being, exists as an end in itself, not merely as a means to be used by this or that will at its discretion. [52]

The case of forced labour during the Nazi period is a cautionary example of what happens when people are treated as a mere means to some arbitrarily appointed end and are compelled to serve the maximization of the 'utility' of society as a whole. This utilitarian worldview also involves a risk of the older members of a society – people perhaps unfit for work or otherwise disabled – being written off as 'underperformers' detracting from, rather than adding to, 'the benefit of the greatest number' and thereby as superfluous, or even as obstructive, to the broader social good. The Nazis put such utilitarian notions as these into practice with frightful logical consistency, carrying out programmes of euthanasia for people with disabilities.

We can already see from just these few examples that utilitarianism has to be rejected as a universally valid moral principle. It is not only unsuitable as such; it is even highly dangerous. Kant leaves his readers in no doubt that, although moral action must indeed always be action which aims at the welfare of all humanity, this must never result in the individual human being's being used as just a means to this noble end; the individual person is, for Kant, always *an end in themselves* with their own inviolable personal dignity:

So act that you use humanity, whether in your own person or in the person of any other, always at the same time as an end, never merely as a means. [53]

The Critique of 'Eudaemonism': Virtue Alone is Not Enough

One of the oldest ethical concepts is *'eudaemonism'*. This ethical principle is traceable back to Aristotle and proposes that a human being should act in such a manner that his actions acquire for him a condition of *eudaemonia*. This Greek word has been variously rendered into English as 'happiness', 'welfare', and 'human flourishing'. To the extent that it can be translated as 'happiness', this recommendation for human action may appear, at first, to be barely different from the 'hedonistic' recommendation of Epicurus, which also sets the happiness of the individual as the goal of ethics. Aristotle's *eudaemonia*, however, is really a very different thing from Epicurus's *hedone*. Whereas *hedone* evokes 'happiness' simply in the sense of the enjoyment of pleasure through the physical senses, *eudaemonia* evokes a more enduring, inward, spiritual happiness and contentment.

A state of *eudaemonia* is also something that is much harder to acquire than a state of mere hedonistic pleasure. In order to achieve that feeling of enduring inward contentedness and satisfaction that *eudaemonia* evokes, an individual has to 'work on himself', with vigour and determination, over an extended period. The 'happiness' at issue here is a state of being perfectly in harmony with oneself and a human being can only achieve this by developing and deploying all his potential virtues. These virtues are many. Moreover, the deployment of a human virtue involves, in each case, first discovering a 'golden mean'. Thus, courage, as a cardinal virtue, is the 'golden mean' between cowardice and recklessness; self-confidence the 'golden mean' between conceitedness and self-abasement; and generosity the 'golden mean' between profligacy and avarice. But Aristotle also counts friendship as a virtue, or commitment to promoting the welfare of all. "That man is happy who constantly acts virtuously," writes Aristotle in the *Nicomachean Ethics*. And Kant certainly appears to agree with Aristotle that the development of the virtues is a very important thing:

Understanding, wit, judgment and the like, whatever such talents of mind may be called, or courage, resolution and perseverance in one's plans [...] are undoubtedly good and desirable for many purposes [...]. [54]

Thus, an upright and proper man can, through his understanding, his decisiveness and his courage, bring about much that is good, and can even render heroic service to his fellow men. And where he does so, he has developed his personal virtues for the greater welfare of all. But this, warns Kant, is unfortunately just one of the many possible ways in which personal virtues can be developed, because:

[...] (these talents) can also be extremely evil and harmful if the will which is to make use of these gifts of nature [...] is not good. [55]

Kant advances against Aristotle here the provocative thesis that, even where virtues are present, they are still no guarantee that a person's actions will be morally good. Virtues, argues Kant, possess no essentially moral quality in themselves. They are, indeed, often 'double-edged'. Such virtues as courage or coolly calculating intellect can be applied not only by a policeman but also by a cold-blooded bank-robber, and in the latter case will do harm rather than good to society:

For without the basic principles of a good will they can become extremely evil, and the coolness of a scoundrel makes him not only far more dangerous but also immediately more abominable in our eyes than we would have taken him to be without it. [56]

But Kant does not just criticize the deployment of virtues as an insufficient basis for a universal principle of moral action; his view of *'eudaemonism'* is generally a deeply sceptical one. Because the goal of this *'eudaemonism'* is individual contentment – that is to say, an inward self-satisfaction such as can be achieved through consistently virtuous patterns of action. Kant, however, considers this inward self-satisfaction to be a very precarious thing. There will always exist in the virtuous individual a temptation to become arrogant, particularly where his virtues have brought him fame and honour:

Honour, even health, and that complete wellbeing and satisfaction with one's condition called happiness, produce boldness and thereby often arrogance as well, unless a good will is present which corrects the influence of these on the mind and, in so doing, also corrects the whole principle of action [...]. 57

Gifted people who possess many virtues have, Kant believes, a greater tendency to arrogance than other, less gifted individuals. Conversely, people less richly equipped by Nature with intelligence, courage and the other virtues may nonetheless act in a morally good way, even if their capacities are extremely limited. For Kant, the decisive thing here is their good will alone. Thus he writes, in an especially emphatic passage:

Even if, by a special disfavour of fortune or by the niggardly provision of a stepmotherly Nature, this will should wholly

lack the capacity to carry out its purpose – if with its greatest efforts it should yet achieve nothing and only the good will were left [...] – then, like a jewel, it would still shine by itself, as something which has its full worth in itself. [58]

For Kant, then, there counts, in the end, nothing but the good will. Because it is this good will alone which decides whether Aristotle's 'virtues' are applied in the right way or the wrong. But how does Kant believe such a 'good will' to be established? From what point on does a 'good will' become 'good'? How can we measure its goodness? Does a will become 'good' simply by willingly obeying existing laws?

The Critique of Legalism: Laws Can Be Unjust

The fourth great ethical principle is indeed 'legalism', named from the Latin word 'legalis' which translates as 'in accordance with the law' or 'allowed by law'. This principle dictates that every action is legal which accords with the law. Legalism as an ethical principle requires of people that they abide, in every case, by existing laws and avoid all infringements of these latter. A 'legalistic imperative' would run: 'So act that your actions always comply with the law'.

By 'the law', however, is meant here not only state law but religious law as well. A Christian who obeys the Ten Commandments can also be said to be following a legalistic form of ethics. Legalism is certainly, in modern societies, an important foundation for our moral orientation. We learn already during childhood what is allowed and what is forbidden and what rules and laws we need to comply with. Indeed, it is only because we commit ourselves, from childhood on, to complying in our everyday lives with this legalistic principle of behaving in conformity with existing laws that our society functions at all. For example, if people did not generally voluntarily comply with the rule 'thou shalt not steal', no shop would be able to offer its goods for sale. The number of crimes of theft, fraud and even murder committed would hugely outweigh the number solved. If a whole nation were to set aside that obligation which we voluntarily lay upon ourselves to be honest and to respect the property of others, and were only to pay for things needed or wanted in cases where the theft of these things, or their acquisition by fraud, would be likely to be discovered, then social chaos would be inevitable.

Legalism, then, is an important moral principle and Kant recognizes this himself. Still, he considers legalism to be unsuitable as a supreme law governing moral action. Legalism, argues Kant, is a 'heteronomous' morality of commandments. This term 'heteronomous' is another word of Greek origin, with *heteros* meaning 'other' or 'external', and *nomos*, meaning 'law'. When we act legalistically we follow a moral principle which addresses us, as it were, from somewhere *outside* our own selves; our moral action is prescribed to us, as law, by some authority external to our own person – be this authority the Bible, the Koran, the Talmud, or the lawbooks of some national or international government. The great drawback in such legalism is clear: a heteronomous ethics of laws and commandments is only as good as the laws by which it is formed. If the laws themselves are bad, then the acts that ensue from abiding by them will necessarily be so too. An extreme example of this is given by the executions of civilians which were carried out in the Second World War on the orders of superior officers. Those soldiers prosecuted, due to such acts, as war criminals usually offered a defence on legalistic principles, saying that they were not guilty since they were only following orders or abiding by the laws and regulations of the time.

In medieval times crusades were justified by citing passages from the Bible. And still today devout Christians sometimes refuse blood transfusions which could save lives, abiding by what appears to be commanded in a biblical text (*Acts* 15:20) about avoiding contamination through unchastity and strange blood.

It is for such reasons that Kant warns against trusting, for one's ethics, exclusively to laws and commandments. Even when, as in this last case, the commandment is held to come from God Himself or from one of his prophets or evangelists we may not, argues Kant, simply execute it and entrust our moral lives to legalism:

> So far as practical reason has the right to lead us, we will not hold actions to be obligatory because they are God's commands but will rather regard them as divine commands because we are internally obligated to them. [59]

But to which of these commands we do in fact render ourselves 'internally obligated' is something we must decide for ourselves. Kant, then, mistrusts legalism as a heteronomous ethics of commands, since it addresses itself to people from a place 'outside them', making them not self-determined but 'other-determined'. It does, indeed, make sense to comply with the laws of the land; but we need always to test the quality of these laws by the measure of a supreme 'inner' moral law. In other words, such a supreme moral law, which allows us to decide what is good and what is evil, can never come from outside us but must rather be something which we generate, autonomously, by ourselves. But is this possible? Can we really judge, out of our own inner resources alone, what is morally good and right? Yes, we can. And this is perhaps the most radical message that Kant's philosophy offers.

The Categorical Imperative – The One True Moral Law

There does in fact exist a way of deciding with absolute certainty, relying on one's own inner mental resources alone, what is good and what is bad in the moral realm. We need no Ten Commandments, no lawbook, no utility-calculus, no feelings of pleasure or unpleasure, nor any Aristotelian list of virtues. Each person can find within himself the touchstone of good and evil. He needs only to hold to that simple recommendation which is by now world-famous: the 'categorical imperative':

So act that the maxim of your will could always hold at the same time as a principle in a giving of universal law. [60]

From the start, Kant was searching for a moral law which, in contrast to the traditional moral conceptions of his predecessors, would be valid *a priori*, i.e. valid independently of any concrete experience.

Everyone must grant that a law, if it is to hold morally, that is, as a ground of an obligation, must carry with it absolute necessity; [...] that,

therefore, the ground of obligation here must not be sought in the nature of the human being or in the circumstances of the world in which he is placed but a priori simply in concepts of pure reason. [61]

A moral law's 'ground of obligation', then, must not be anything derived from experience; it must have its source *a priori* in pure reason. Kant clarifies this using the example of the moral law stated in the King James Bible as 'thou shalt not bear false witness' (in modern language 'you must not lie'). If I justify complying with such a law by citing my experience – saying, for example, that lying has not worked out well for me in the past and that I have had more success by being honest – this is to take a great moral risk. Because then, if my experience ever appears to teach me the opposite lesson – namely, that 'the honest guy loses out' – I will feel this law to be no longer binding on me. This is why any really workable foundation for moral laws must be a foundation independent of people's concrete life-experiences.

For Kant, it followed from this that the supreme moral law could not be derived from existing laws – be they civil or religious - either. Because bodies of civil law or religious scripture themselves contain the traces and results of specific human experiences; their validity is not an *a priori* validity, independent of all experience.

Kant posed, then, the really decisive question, a question whose answer led him straight to the 'categorical imperative': what would a moral law need to look like if it were to possess absolute validity for the actions of every human being, could be complied with by every human being in exactly the same way, and were not imposed on these human beings from some heteronomous 'outside'?

The answer was obvious: this moral law would have to come from within! It would have to be a law which

Man as a rational being imposed upon himself: a kind of self-commitment on the part of the faculty of reason to act always only in such a way that one's actions complied with a moral law which would be at the same time valid for all other people and which could be followed by all these latter. By posing the problem in these terms Kant had already found the solution to it. He needed only to reformulate his own question as an answer and couch this answer in the form of an imperative: You must, by your own free choosing, so act that you can wish the principle of your action to be elevated to the status of a law valid for everyone; or, in Kant's own phrasing:

So act that the maxim of your will could always hold at the same time as a principle in a giving of universal law. [62]

Why does Kant call this recommendation for moral action a categorical imperative? Why not simply 'imperative'? 'Imperative', after all, just means 'command'. It is used, in grammar, to signify that mode of speech which exhorts to a certain action (as in that phrase-type which we have often encountered here: 'So act that ....!'). Why, then, is Kant careful to add the word 'categorical'? He wants to distinguish very clearly, through this word, his own moral principle from that of the utilitarians, who mostly achieved only hypothetical imperatives. A hypothetical imperative is an imperative which applies only under a certain 'if' condition. For example, the imperative 'Stop smoking, if you want to live long and stay healthy!' is a hypothetical imperative. It is valid only if we accept the premiss, or condition, that someone does indeed want to live to a ripe old age. But Kant's imperative, as he strongly insists, is valid always, everywhere, and unconditionally. It is categorical.

> Accordingly, the moral law is [...] an imperative that commands categorically because the law is unconditional. [63]

By this Kant also means that the demands of the moral law allow for no contingencies of human disposition. No importance, for example, must be ascribed to whether, when about to perform a moral action, one experiences feelings of pleasure, aversion, or even fear. As Kant writes:

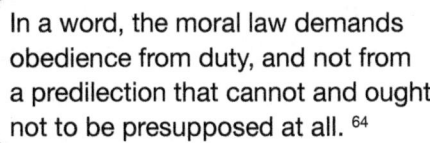

In a word, the moral law demands obedience from duty, and not from a predilection that cannot and ought not to be presupposed at all. [64]

Here once again Kant is taking a firm position against the hedonistic and utilitarian ethical concepts. Whoever acts out of personal inclination, because he expects some gain in pleasure or benefit, is not really acting morally. If, for example, someone falls into the water and calls for help, it must be of no relevance whether the water is cold or whether one is afraid of being drowned oneself. The hedonist would decide whether to act or not on just such grounds of good or bad 'feeling'. The utilitarian might possibly weigh up what reward rescuing the drowning man might get him; he would make his help dependent on a calculation of risk and benefit. The legalist would perhaps jump into the water or fetch help but only due to knowing that 'failure to render assistance' is a prosecutable offence and that he must abide by the law; it is possible, however, that his awareness of this law would cause him to pretend not to have seen the drowning man. The eudaemonist, being a virtuous man, would probably attempt a rescue, since his cultivated virtues may include courage and dedication to the general welfare; but let us hope, for the drowning man's sake, that the *eudaemonist* has not also cultivated other virtues, such as cunning and cleverness to justify inaction.

The drowning man can only be absolutely sure of being helped, then, if he has the luck to be spotted by a passing Kantian. This latter will not hesitate for a second but will jump in and rescue him 'categorically' – i.e. without conditions or extra considerations of any kind. And when the rescued swimmer asks the Kantian why he risked his life to save him, the Kantian will reply: "It was my duty". Indeed the categorical imperative allows only one course of action in this situation: an immediate rescue-attempt. Because it is only such an action that we could possibly want to see raised to the status of a universal law – i.e. the law that anyone who sees a person drowning must immediately try to rescue them, regardless of all feelings, fears, or calculations of likely benefit.

Duty and Free Will

The only motive, then, that Kant accepts as a valid motive for a truly moral action is the *fulfilment of one's duty*. And this duty consists in the voluntary subjection of our free will to the categorical imperative. When writing about 'duty' Kant often falls into a rhapsodic tone that is highly unusual for him:

Duty! Sublime and mighty name that [...] requires submission [...]; what origin is there worthy of you and where is to be found the root of your noble descent, which rejects all kinship with the inclinations, descent from which is the indispensable condition of that worth which human beings alone can give themselves? [65]

Kant finds a truly metaphysical fascination in this question about the origin of duty because duty compels us to ask just what kind of reality we are evoking whenever we use the word 'ought'. (It helps here to bear in mind that the German word for 'ought', *sollen*, is used to formulate both religious commandments – the 'thou shalt' of the King James Bible is, in Luther's German, *'du sollst'* – and also such non-religious prescriptions for moral action as Kant's own categorical imperative.) It is the mere fact that human beings are capable of subjecting our wills to this 'ought' that fascinates Kant enormously. Because it is clearly no use looking for any such thing as an 'ought' in the natural, physical world. If the 'ought' is a reality, it is necessarily a *metaphysical* reality. And it is Man's relation to the 'ought' that gives Man a unique status within the natural world.

The *'ought'* expresses a species of necessity and a connection with grounds which does not occur anywhere else in the whole of Nature. [66]

In non-human Nature, 'ought' is a meaningless word. It makes no sense to say that rivers 'ought' to flow uphill, flowers 'ought not' to bloom, or lions 'ought not' to eat antelopes. In Nature, everything is governed by merely *natural* laws. Effect follows cause in an unbroken chain. Man alone is capable, thanks to his free will, of acting spontaneously in accordance with his own ideas and principles:

Everything in Nature works in accordance with laws. Only a rational being has the capacity to act [...] in accordance with principles, or has a *will*. [67]

Man indeed, as a higher form of mammal, has certain purely natural dispositions and drives such as hunger and thirst. He is also constantly exposed to stimuli affecting his five senses which may exert great influence on his will. But Kant believes that Man, as a rational being, is able at any moment to catapult himself out of the natural chain of stimulus and reaction and to decide to act in accordance with the 'ought' alone:

> However many natural grounds or sensible stimuli there may be that impel me to will, they cannot produce the 'ought'. [68]

That Man is capable at all of hearkening to this 'ought' and following the dictates of the categorical imperative presupposes that the human will is free to decide either for something or against it. Man must be free in his essence because, if he were not, all propositions containing the word 'ought' would be completely meaningless. The freedom of the human will, then, is a necessary transcendental condition of all ethical action. Kant accepts that this freedom of the human will cannot be proven, since it is not perceptible through the senses and therefore cannot be known by theoretical reason. But when considering human beings as subjects of ethical practice we have to assume that this freedom of the will does exist.

We see here very clearly the difference and the interplay between theoretical reason and practical reason. In terms of the theory of knowledge the freedom of the human will is unprovable, since theoretical reason cannot grasp it; but if we are to comprehend real human practice we are bound to assume, as a 'given', that the human will is free, since free will is a necessary precondition of that human practice which consists in moral acts. But it is important to recognize that theoretical and practical reason are just two aspects of a single rational faculty, which adopts two different standpoints to address two different areas of human experience.

Kant, then, in the end harbours no doubt regarding the freedom of the will: Man is free to will what is good and to opt for good over evil. The highest ethical law, therefore, and the perfect ideal of ethical action is the free will's decision to commit and subject itself to the categorical imperative:

It is impossible to think of anything at all in the world, or indeed even beyond it, that could be considered good without limitation except a good will. [69]

Only the good will counts, not the effects it achieves. The effects and results of an action are, from the moral viewpoint, of secondary importance at best. Kant writes:

A good will is not good because of what it effects or accomplishes, because of its fitness to to attain some proposed end, but only because of its willing; that is, it is good in itself. [70]

Thus, from the moral point of view, it is absolutely important to want to jump into the water and rescue the drowning man. Whether the rescue succeeds or not is unimportant, in the end, for the judgment of the deed's moral quality. The decisive thing is the good will of the individual performing it.

What May I Hope?
The Critique of Religion

To the question: 'is the categorical imperative derived from the idea of God?' Kant's answer was: it is really the other way around: if there is a God, then He, above all, is bound to comply with the categorical imperative; for God Himself is only an idea derived from this imperative:

> The idea of such a being, before whom all knees bow, emerges from this imperative and not the reverse. [71]

The same applies to Jesus, whom the Gospels proclaim to be the holy Son of God:

> Even the Holy One of the Gospels must first be compared with our ideal of moral perfection before he is cognized as such. [72]

In one of his shorter publications, which bears the significant title *Religion within the Boundaries of Mere Reason*, Kant defines moral action in accordance with the moral law alone as an autonomous act of the free human will, which thereby chooses to orient itself toward the Good. All other actions which the church may demand beyond this, such as acts of penitence and other rituals, he sharply rejects, as in the following passage:

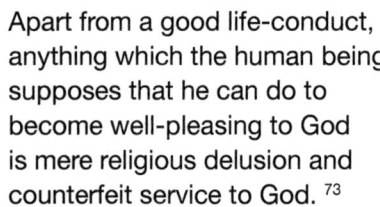

Apart from a good life-conduct, anything which the human being supposes that he can do to become well-pleasing to God is mere religious delusion and counterfeit service to God. [73]

In the last analysis all religion must expose itself to the question of its reasonableness – i.e. the question of whether it fulfils, within the limits of reason alone, a meaningful and morally justifiable function of the sort defined by the categorical imperative. Kant thereby marked off the limits of the sphere within which religion could be allowed to persist within an enlightened society. On the condition that belief in God helps to realize the supreme moral law of practical reason, such belief is to be welcomed – but *only* on this condition. He answers the question: 'what may I hope?' by replacing religious revelation with what he calls the 'postulates of reason'. But these 'postulates' are, as the term suggests in its original Latin meaning, no more than 'demands' or 'recommendations' of reason. That is to say, it may, within limits, serve the cause of practical reason to accept the idea of the immortality of the soul or even of God as a principle of moral goodness, although it is impossible to cognize or to prove such ideas. But this does not mean that these ideas are *necessary* to morality. Kant leaves us in no doubt about this:

Morality [...] is in need neither of the idea of another being above (the individual human being) in order that (this latter) recognize his duty, nor, in order that he observe it, of an incentive other than the (moral) law itself [...]. [74]

We can, then, only be sure of the rightness of our moral actions if we rely exclusively on our own good will and freely obligate ourselves to 'good action' as defined by the categorical imperative. As the cultural historian Egon Friedell once put it: as a knowing being Man is law-maker for the world outside and around him; as a moral being he is law-maker for himself.

Of What Use Is Kant's Discovery for Us Today?

The Foundation of the Sciences

Kant's 'critical philosophy' was a great turning point in the history of our world, the effects of which we still feel today. One might say that there was a 'world before Kant' and a 'world after Kant'. Whereas the world that existed before Kant's 'critical philosophy' was still a naïve one, in which human knowledge was a confused mass of overlapping realms and spheres and different claims of access to truth, our 'post-Kantian' world is marked by a clear and irreversible division of the sciences and of their respective realms of competence. Kant defined, for the first time, four great realms of scientific knowledge and divided these from one another in the most precise way. He succeeded in separating, once and for all, philosophy from theology; in establishing a firm basis for modern mathematics and physics; and in laying, moreover, the foundation stone for the whole corpus of the modern natural sciences.

Even today the church has not entirely forgiven Kant for his separating of philosophy from theology. The Kantian 'critique of knowledge' has been accused of discrediting theology, the 'science of God', and banishing it into the realm of mere speculation. Kant had already in his own lifetime to defend himself against this charge, writing in self-justification that:

I had to deny knowledge in order to make room for faith [...]. [75]

There is no doubt that Kant did indeed, in his *Critique of Pure Reason*, assign to religious faith a realm of its own that lay beyond the realm of knowledge. But this does not invalidate the accusation that, precisely by drawing such a sharp dividing line between the realm of faith and that of knowledge, Kant became 'religion's gravedigger'. Modern Man has tended, in ever greater numbers, to rely on knowledge rather than faith. At the very centre of this 'knowledge' to which modern Man entrusts his fate stand the natural sciences. And these too, in their modern form, are inseparably bound up with the name of Kant. It was Kant who fired, as it were, the starting pistol for that great race for truth between researchers and engineers in many fields that began at the end of the 18th Century. His revolutionary 'critique of knowledge' created for the first time clarity regarding proper scientific method. Kant established the requirement that, even though theories can be formed *a priori*, natural-scientific knowledge must always be testable on the basis of the data provided by the senses. This laid the foundation stone for experimental physics. Regardless of whether a theoretical model happens to be generated via observation or, conversely, observation of natural phenomena is conducted through the prism of an already-formed theory, knowledge must in both cases be empirical, i.e. grounded in repeatable experiments. Once this strict premiss was accepted, results achieved by researchers all over the world became mutually comparable and the triumphal march of modern technology could begin.

The Categorical Imperative – The Spur to Morality

Kant's categorical imperative has been, for over two hundred years now, the object of much discussion, praise, veneration and sometimes also criticism. At the beginning of the last century, for example, the German philosopher Max Scheler criticized the 'abstract' character of Kant's imperative, arguing that real values and concrete substance, such as a commitment to human rights, were not to be found in it. Instead of Kant's formal ethics we need, Scheler argued, a "material value-ethics". In recent years, however, such criticism is heard less often. It has been recognized that the categorical imperative does implicitly comprise certain very concrete commitments, as when Kant writes:

Now I say that the human being and in general every rational being exists as an end in itself, not merely as a means to be used by this or that will at its discretion. [76]

This apparently abstract formulation in fact contains the proposition that every human being is a person and must be respected. A person must not be misused as a mere means to an end but is rather in himself the very highest of ends, as is humanity in its entirety. This in turn implies that each individual has a right to the development of his own personality according to his own aims and goals. The second version of the categorical imperative which Kant derives from the first clearly confirms this:

So act that you use humanity, whether in your own person or in the person of any other, always at the same time as an end, never merely as a means. [77]

The practical maxim outlined here is one that demands not only that we respect mankind understood as consisting of individual personalities with correspondent individual rights, but also that we recognize that all these individual persons who make up mankind enjoy absolute equality with one another. There is, then, even now no substantial criticism that can fairly be levelled against the categorical imperative. It remains the human race's best possible practical maxim and contains in itself that cosmopolitan moral self-conception which we are still today working toward making a concrete global reality.

Kant was admired for this achievement by his contemporaries, especially by the writers and poets of the age. Some, however, expressed reservations about the way in which the strict-minded philosopher elevated 'duty' above all other moral motives. Already many of Kant's contemporaries were repelled, for example, by Kant's argument that a benefactor of others who happens to feel inner pleasure at his own kind acts is not really acting morally, since he is acting out of 'inclination' rather than duty:

> But I assert that in such a case an action of this kind [...] has nevertheless no true moral worth [...] for the maxim lacks moral content, namely, that of doing such actions not from inclination but from duty. [78]

These lines prompted the poet Friedrich Schiller to compose a short poem mocking this exalted Kantian idea of duty:

"'When I do good for friends, I do it gladly
But fear this means from virtue I'm exempt'
'None does his duty who feels glad to do it!
Learn, then, to serve your fellows
with contempt!'" [79]

Kant, it is true, formulated his ethical ideas in a language of dismaying rigour. If nothing that we feel *inclined* to do can count as moral, there will be precious few 'moral acts' left in most people's lives. But Kant himself conceded that it is not possible to satisfy, always and everywhere, the rigorous demands of the categorical imperative. This imperative is rather an ethical *ideal* which constantly spurs us on to aim higher. Moreover – and this is the most important message of Kant's moral philosophy – every human being is in a position to decide for himself what is morally good. No one may, and no one must, carry out commands for which they cannot themselves take responsibility. Kant indeed never formulated – as did, for example, John Locke – an explicit right to civil disobedience. But there is really no other conclusion to be drawn from Kant's categorical imperative but that the individual is bound to reject any law, order or commandment of questionable conformity with the inward moral law which this imperative represents. Because in the last analysis we are responsible to no one but ourselves. We bear the supreme moral law within us. The whole world around us must bear being measured by its standard.

Sustainability – the Maxim of the Modern Age

Consistent application of the categorical imperative has never been as important as it is today. Whether key industrial nations will agree, at climate summit meetings, on a reduction in carbon and other emissions; whether billions of private households will commit themselves to sustainable daily practices – the answers to these questions depend upon whether we can follow Kant in coordinating the principles which govern our individual actions with the action of humanity as a whole. As long as individual states and citizens give precedence, in utilitarian manner, to their own benefit over solutions that are valid as universal models, the plunder of the natural bases of our existence will continue. A philosopher today is sometimes tempted to pursue Kant's project of enlightenment so far as to demand that heads of state be compelled, before each such summit meeting, to take part in philosophical training sessions at whose end they would be able not just to recite but to apply the categorical imperative:

So act that you use humanity [...] always at the same time as an end, never merely as a means. [80]

Mostly, politicians as representatives of national economic interests obey no imperative but the following: 'So act that you secure the survival and prosperity of your own nation, using other nations as mere means to this end by persuading them to voluntarily reduce their own emissions while, so as to protect your own national economic interest, agreeing to the minimum possible degree of such reduction yourself'. The key lesson of enlightenment – that we need to think and to act in a way that transcends individual personal and individual national interest – is understood by many people today but seldom put into practice. There still applies, then, to our era what Kant said of his own: the critical impulse of enlightenment is still far from having completed its task and

> if it is now asked whether we at present live in an enlightened age, the answer is: 'No, but we do live in an age of enlightenment'. [81]

Kant's warning to his contemporaries that the project of enlightenment needed to be pursued further is one that definitely bears repeating today in the face of the challenge of finding new ways to manage our relations with the planet we live on. Is it not, however, already too late? Can ecological collapse still be prevented? The philosopher Adorno feared that 'objective reason' has already been completely displaced by 'instrumental reason' and that mankind today has fallen helplessly under the sway of global capitalism's calculations of short-term profit and selfish interest. The project of enlightenment, Adorno claims, is doomed to failure. This was not Kant's view. He believed that a turn from unreason toward reason is always possible for Man in principle, and can be effected at any time:

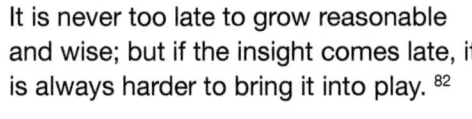

It is never too late to grow reasonable and wise; but if the insight comes late, it is always harder to bring it into play. [82]

It must be admitted that Man really has arrived only very late at the insight that we must relate sustainably to our planet. Since time immemorial we have been used to plundering the earth's resources. But the biblical command to exercise 'dominion over the earth' must now give way to a new critical thinking. And if there is any ethical principle in the whole history of philosophy which offers absolute support to the new ecological ideal of 'sustainability', it is surely Kant's categorical imperative.

Enlightenment Never Ends - Sapere Aude!

Kant is the key thinker of the 'Age of Enlightenment', that epoch which spread a new way of thinking to people all over Europe. In France Rousseau, Montesquieu and Diderot raised the demand that medieval unreason, with its witch-burnings, exorcisms and 'divine right of kings', be forced finally to give way to modern, rational thinking and a democratic state. In England, writers like Locke and Hume lent their pens to the same cultural and political causes. Kant, in Prussia, was fully aware of what a watershed in history he was living through:

Enlightenment is the human being's emergence from his self-incurred minority. [83]

What Kant calls mankind's 'minority' here – meaning the condition of being like 'minors', i.e. like children – he saw to be 'self-incurred' inasmuch as humanity had left its innate powers of reason unused for far too long. For centuries, Kant argued, human beings had lived fearful lives under the constraint of religion and superstition, never posing critical questions regarding either social or natural forces:

This minority is self-incurred when its cause lies not in lack of understanding but in lack of [...] courage to use it [...]. [84]

People had lacked courage to question ruling dogmas. Thus, 'divine right' had long remained unchallenged and the king accepted just because he was the son of the last king. Only with the French Revolution did change begin. From then on the cry was taken up: 'Rule for the people by the people'. Although Kant lived in the monarchical state of Prussia he too demanded the critical examination of all traditions and dogmas. He included already in the preface to the *Critique of Pure Reason* the oft-cited lines which reflect the sense of radical new beginnings in the air:

> Our age is the genuine age of criticism, to which everything must submit. Religion, through its holiness, and legislation, through its majesty, commonly seek to exempt themselves from it. But in this way they excite a just suspicion against themselves and cannot lay claim to [...] unfeigned respect [...]. [85]

He adds that such 'unfeigned respect' is deserved only by 'that which has been able to withstand free and public examination (by reason)'. We must, then, in principle doubt every law and put it to reason's test. And if it does not stand up under such examination, then it must be improved or abolished, for:

> This much is certain: whosoever has once tasted of critique forever loathes all the dogmatic chatter [...]. [86]

This call for permanent critique of what exists is still applicable to our present age and is perhaps the most important part of Kant's legacy to us. We must never cease examining and questioning the *status quo*. The stirring words with which Kant exhorts his readers to critical thought are more relevant today than they ever were:

Sapere aude! Have courage to make use of your *own* understanding! [87]

Bibliographical References

The quotations from Kant are all drawn from the current standard English-language edition of the philosopher's works, The Cambridge Edition of the Works of Immanuel Kant (Cambridge University Press).

1   Kant, Critique of Practical Reason, in Practical Philosophy,
    CE (hereinafter 'CE'), p. 269
2   Kant, Critique of Pure Reason, CE, p. 639
3   Kant, Critique of Pure Reason, CE, p. 101
4   Kant, Critique of Pure Reason, CE, p. 193
5   Kant, Lectures on Logic, CE, p. 538
6   Kant, Anthropology From a Pragmatic Point of View,
    in Anthropology, History and Education, CE, p. 405
7   Kant, What is Enlightenment? in Practical Philosophy, CE, p. 17
8   Kant, Critique of Pure Reason, CE, p. 101
9   Kant, Critique of Pure Reason, CE, p. 117
10 Kant, Critique of Pure Reason, CE, p. 668
11 Kant, Critique of Pure Reason, CE, p.136
12 Kant, Critique of Pure Reason, CE, pps. 193-4
13 Kant, Critique of Pure Reason, CE, ibid.
14 Kant, Critique of Pure Reason, CE, ibid.
15 Kant, Critique of Pure Reason, CE, p. 136
16 Kant, Critique of Pure Reason, CE, ibid.
17 Kant, Critique of Pure Reason, CE, ibid.
18 Kant, Critique of Pure Reason, CE, ibid.
19 Kant, Critique of Pure Reason, CE, p. 157
20 Kant, Critique of Pure Reason, CE, p. 158
21 Kant, Critique of Pure Reason, CE, p. 158
22 Kant, Critique of Pure Reason, CE, p. 157
23 Kant, Critique of Pure Reason, CE, p. 158
24 Kant, Critique of Pure Reason, CE, p. 178
25 Kant, Critique of Pure Reason, CE, p. 181
26 Kant, Critique of Pure Reason, CE, p. 185
27 Kant, Critique of Pure Reason, CE, p. 185
28 Kant, Critique of Pure Reason, CE, p. 384

29   Kant, Critique of the Power of Judgement, CE, p.66
30   Kant, Critique of Pure Reason, CE, p. 206
31   Kant, Critique of Pure Reason, CE, p. 212
32   Kant, Critique of Pure Reason, CE, p. 213
33   Kant, Critique of Pure Reason, CE, p. 246
34   Kant, Critique of Pure Reason, CE, p. 247
35   Kant, The False Subtlety of the Four Syllogistic Figures in
       Theoretical Philosophy 1755-1770, CE, p. 89
36   Kant, Critique of Pure Reason, CE, p. 214
37   Kant, Critique of Pure Reason, CE, p. 252
38   Kant, Critique of Pure Reason, CE, p. 110
39   Kant, Dreams of a Spirit-Seer Elucidated by Dreams of Metaphysics,
       in Theoretical Philosophy 1755-1770, CE, p. 344
40   Kant, Critique of Pure Reason, CE, p. 254
41   Kant, Critique of Pure Reason, CE, pps. 621-622
42   Kant, Critique of Pure Reason, CE, p. 672
43   Kant, Critique of Pure Reason, CE, p. 586
44   Kant, Critique of Practical Reason, in Practical Philosophy,
       CE, p. 207
45   Kant, Critique of the Power of Judgment, CE, pps. 146-7
46   Kant, Critique of Pure Reason, CE, p. 99
47   Kant, Critique of Pure Reason, CE, p. 387
48   Kant, Critique of Practical Reason, in Practical Philosophy,
       CE, p. 164
49   Kant, Groundwork of the Metaphysics of Morals,
       in Practical Philosophy, CE, p. 45
50   Kant, Critique of Practical Reason, in Practical Philosophy,
       CE, p. 155
51   Kant, Critique of Practical Reason, in Practical Philosophy,
       CE, p. 266
52   Kant, Groundwork of the Metaphysics of Morals,
       in Practical Philosophy, CE, p. 79
53   Kant, Groundwork of the Metaphysics of Morals,
       in Practical Philosophy, CE, p. 80
54   Kant, Groundwork of the Metaphysic of Morals,
       in Practical Philosophy, CE, p. 49
55   Kant, Groundwork of the Metaphysics of Morals,
       in Practical Philosophy, CE, ibid.

56   Kant, Groundwork of the Metaphysics of Morals,
     in Practical Philosophy, CE, p. 50
57   Kant, Groundwork of the Metaphysics of Morals,
     in Practical Philosophy, CE, p. 49
58   Kant, Groundwork of the Metaphysics of Morals,
     in Practical Philosophy, CE, p. 50
59   Kant, Critique of Pure Reason, CE, p. 684
60   Kant, Critique of Practical Reason,
     in Practical Philosophy, CE, p. 164
61   Kant, Groundwork of Metaphysics of Morals,
     in Practical Philosophy, CE, p. 44
62   Kant, Critique of Practical Reason,
     in Practical Philosophy, CE, p. 164
63   Kant, Critique of Practical Reason,
     in Practical Philosophy, CE, p. 165
64   Kant, Critique of Practical Reason,
     in Practical Philosophy, CE, p. 266
65   Kant, Critique of Practical Reason,
     in Practical Philosophy, CE, p. 209
66   Kant, Critique of Pure Reason, CE, p. 540
67   Kant, Groundwork of the Metaphysics of Morals,
     in Practical Philosophy, CE, p. 66
68   Kant, Critique of Pure Reason, CE, p. 541
69   Kant, Groundwork of the Metaphysic of Morals,
     in Practical Philosophy, CE, p. 49
70   Kant, Groundwork of the Metaphysics of Morals,
     in Practical Philosophy, CE, p. 50
71   Kant, Opus Postumum, CE, p. 204
72   Kant, Groundwork of the Metaphysics of Morals,
     in Practical Philosophy, CE, p. 63
73   Kant, Religion Within the Boundaries of Mere Reason,
     in Religion and Rational Theology, Cambridge, p. 166
74   Kant, Religion Within the Boundaries of Mere Reason,
     in Religion and Rational Theology, Cambridge, p. 33
75   Kant, Critique of Pure Reason, Cambridge, p. 117
76   Kant, Groundwork of the Metaphysics of Morals,
     in Practical Philosophy, CE, p. 79

77   Kant, Groundwork of the Metaphysics of Morals,
     in Practical Philosophy, CE, p. 80
78   Kant, Groundwork of the Metaphysics of Morals,
     in Practical Philosophy, CE, p. 53
79   This little couplet was one of the satirical verses that Schiller
     published together with his friend Goethe in the collection Xenien
     in 1797.
80   Kant, Groundwork of the Metaphysics of Morals,
     in Practical Philosophy, CE, p. 80
81   Kant, What Is Enlightenment? in Practical Philosophy, CE, p. 21
82   Kant, Prolegomena to Any Future Metaphysics,
     in Theoretical Philosophy After 1781, CE, p. 54
83   Kant, What Is Enlightenment? in Practical Philosophy, CE, p. 17.
     (On the meaning of 'minority' here, see footnote 7 above).
84   Kant, What Is Enlightenment? in Practical Philosophy, CE, ibid.
85   Kant, Critique of Pure Reason, CE, pps. 100-101
86   Kant, Prolegomena to Any Future Metaphysics,
     in Theoretical Philosophy After 1781, CE, p. 154
87   Kant, What Is Enlightenment? in Practical Philosophy, CE, p. 17

Already published in the same series:

Walther Ziegler
Camus in 60 Minutes
ISBN 9783741227738

Walther Ziegler
Freud in 60 Minutes
ISBN 9783741227707

Walther Ziegler
Hegel in 60 Minutes
ISBN 9783741227677

Walther Ziegler
Heidegger in 60 Minutes
ISBN 9783741227752

Walther Ziegler
Kant in 60 Minutes
ISBN 9783741226373

Walther Ziegler
Marx in 60 Minutes
ISBN 9783741227691

Walther Ziegler
Platon in 60 Minutes
ISBN 9783741227615

Walther Ziegler
Rousseau in 60 Minutes
ISBN 9783741227622

Walther Ziegler
Sartre in 60 Minutes
ISBN 9783741227653

Walther Ziegler
Smith in 60 Minutes
ISBN 9783741227721

Coming soon in the same series:

Walther Ziegler
Adorno in 60 Minutes

Walther Ziegler
Arendt in 60 Minutes

Walther Ziegler
Bacon in 60 Minutes

Walther Ziegler
Descartes in 60 Minutes

Walther Ziegler
Foucault in 60 Minutes

Walther Ziegler
Habermas in 60 Minutes

Walther Ziegler
Hobbes in 60 Minutes

Walther Ziegler
Nietzsche in 60 Minutes

Walther Ziegler
Popper in 60 Minutes

Walther Ziegler
Rawls in 60 Minutes

Walther Ziegler
Schopenhauer in 60 Minutes

Walther Ziegler
Wittgenstein in 60 Minutes

The author:

Dr Walther Ziegler is academically trained in the fields of philosophy, history and political science. As a foreign correspondent, reporter and newsroom coordinator for the German TV station ProSieben he has produced films on every continent. His news reports have won several prizes and awards.He has also authored numerous books in the field of philosophy. His many years of experience as a journalist mean that he is able to present the complex ideas of the great philosophers in a way that is both engaging and very clear. Since 2007 he has also been active as a teacher and trainer of young TV journalists in Munich, holding the post of Academic Director at the Media Academy, an institute of higher education that offers film and TV courses at its base directly on the site of the major European film production company Bavaria Film.